Simply The Bible

Nick Page

Illustrations by Jonathan Williams

LION

Published by Lion Books
an imprint of
Lion Hudson plc
Wilkinson House, Jordan Hill Road,
Oxford OX2 8DR, England
www.lionhudson.com/lion

ISBN 978 0 7459 5523 0

First edition 2013

Acknowledgments
Scripture quotations are taken from the *Holy Bible, New International Version.* Copyright © 1978, 1984 by International Bible Society. Used by permission of Hodder & Stoughton, a division of Hodder Headline Ltd. All rights reserved. "NIV" is a registered trademark of International Bible Society. UK trademark number 1448790.

A catalogue record for this book is available from the British Library

Printed and bound in China, March 2013, LH06

Contents

The books

ABOUT THIS BOOK

This book aims to give you a bite-size introduction to every book of the Bible. (With a nibble-sized introduction to each book of the Apocrypha thrown in for free.) But when you've read about the book, why not have a go at reading the Bible yourself? There are lots of good modern translations available. And to get you started, for each book we've even included some suggested readings to help you explore it – what could be more simple!

What is it?

It's a library. Or it's an anthology. Anyway, it's not just one book, it's an anthology of many different kinds of books or writing, including history, poetry, stories, legal codes, proverbs and sayings, apocalyptic visionary descriptions, hymns, letters... It's a book full of books. That's where the name comes from, from the Greek – *ta biblia* – meaning "the books".

Surprise me !

The chapters and verse of the Bible were not in the original text. Our system of chapters dates back to the thirteenth century AD; the verse divisions to the sixteenth century AD.

What's in it?

Sixty-six books bound into one volume.
These are grouped into two sections:

The Old Testament or Hebrew Scriptures (39 books)	The New Testament or Christian Scriptures (27 books)
The Old Testament or Hebrew Scriptures (39 books) – containing writings sacred to both Jews and Christians. This section contains history, prophecy, wisdom, and what some people call the "Pentateuch" or the "Books of the Law". The books in this section were originally written in Hebrew, with some passages in Aramaic.	The New Testament or Christian Scriptures (27 books) – containing writings sacred only to Christians. The New Testament is divided into two main sections: the Gospels and Acts, and the Letters, from people such as Paul, John, and Peter. The books in this section were originally written in Greek, with occasional phrases in Aramaic and Latin.

Apocrypha !

Some Bibles feature a third section known as the Apocrypha. Catholic and Orthodox Bibles include these texts, but most Protestant Bibles do not.

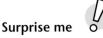

- The books in the Bible were compiled and written by many different people and across thousands of years. "Testament" means "promise". Christians believe that the Old Testament tells the story of God's promise to the Israelites, while the New Testament of his promise to all people.
- The first Christians did not have "the Bible" as we know it. When the early Christians talked about scripture, they were talking about the Hebrew Scriptures, or what we know as the Old Testament. The early Church probably sang Psalms and read the prophets to see how they pointed to Jesus.
- To help people find their way around the text, each book of the Bible is broken down into chapters; and each chapter into verses. In total there are 1,189 chapters and the whole thing rolls in at well over 750,000 words.

Surprise me !

The first person to use *ta biblia* to describe the scriptures was Clement of Alexandria, writing around AD 215. And he was only talking about the Hebrew scriptures. The first recorded use of *ta biblia* to include both Christian and Jewish Scriptures comes from around AD 223. Jerome, writing in the fourth century AD, used the term *bibliotheca* which means "library" or "collection of books" and this was the common term used for centuries among Latin speakers.

Why does it matter?

The Bible is the most important book ever written. No book has exerted more influence on the world – certainly the western world. Art, literature, politics, architecture, history, law – they've all been influenced by the Bible. More importantly, as the basis of two of the great religions of the world, its writings are considered sacred. Christians believe that the Bible is inspired by God, which means that the people who wrote it were passing on messages from God – messages that were not only for the people of their time, but for all people, everywhere and in any time.

The Bible is all about the big issues in life. It addresses fundamental questions: why we're here, where we all came from, what we're supposed to be doing with our lives, how we should treat other people. It talks about real people with real problems – and although they lived a long time ago, they faced exactly the same kind of problems that we face today.

Most of all, Christians believe the Bible speaks to us. It is one of the ways that we hear from God and understand more about him.

In the beginning

What is it?

Very big and very old. It's the opening scene, the start of everything. If this were a film it would be one of those special-effects-driven epics. This book has it all: worlds being created, cities being destroyed, cataclysmic floods, people turned into pillars of salt, famine, death, and disaster.

Starring: Adam, Eve, Noah, Abraham, Sarah, Isaac, Rebekah, Esau, Jacob, Judah, and Joseph

@ GENESIS

In the beginning: God. The epic story of the origins of the human race, their fall and how God starts the rescue plan. This book has everything!

What happens?

We start with the earth, formless and shapeless. Then God speaks and the whole thing is created ❶. Adam and Eve are told they can eat anything, except for the fruit of one tree – so of course that's what they do, inspired by a strange being described as a serpent. After that, creation is broken and they have to leave Eden ❷. We then see the beginnings of civilization: cities get built; music and technology are invented. But sin spreads and the world is evil, so God sends a flood to wash it clean ❸. That's the first part of the book.

In the second part God works through several key figures known as "the patriarchs", which means "the fathers". The first of these is Abraham ❹. God makes promises (known as "covenants") with them ❺. God gives the land of Canaan to Abraham. God destroys Sodom and Gomorrah, but Abraham's nephew, Lot, is rescued (although his wife is turned into a pillar of salt) ❻. Abraham's grandson, Jacob, is a trickster who cheats his brother out of his inheritance. On the run, he has a vision of a ladder reaching up to heaven ❼.

Later, returning home after many years, he wrestles with God and is given the name "Israel" ❽. His son Joseph is hated by his brothers and secretly sold into slavery in Egypt ❾. However, he rises to power and, when famine hits the land many years later, his brothers and their father go to Egypt, where Joseph provides for them ❿.

IN TEN

❶ Creation: 1:1 – 2:4
❷ Adam and Eve: 2:7 – 3:24
❸ Noah: 6:5 – 9:17
❹ Abram's calling: 12:1–7; 13:14–18
❺ Covenant: 15:7–21; 17:1 – 18:15
❻ Sodom and Gomorrah: 18:16 – 19:29
❼ Jacob's ladder: 28:10–22
❽ Call me Israel: 32:1–31
❾ Joseph: 37:1–36; 39:1–21
❿ In Egypt: 41:1 – 50:26

Why does it matter?

Genesis is a "why" book. It's about where we came from and why we are here. It's one of the most important books of the Bible because it introduces many of the themes that run through the entire Bible story: creation, sin, love, sacrifice, judgment – they're all in here. But Genesis is also about the relationship between God and humanity. God is personal. He speaks, he thinks, he relates to humans. He makes a covenant or promise to be with his people and to give them the land.

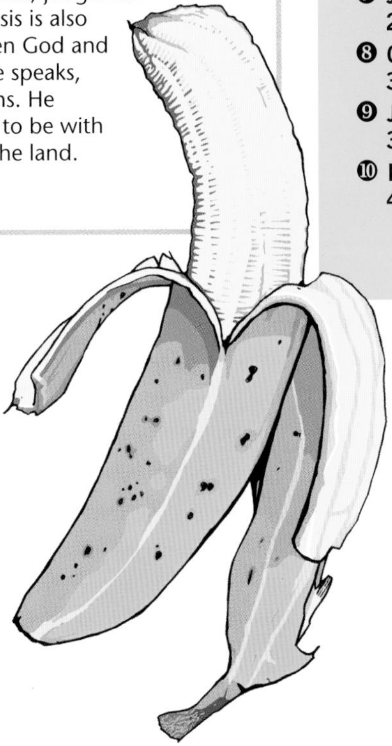

Surprise me

Although traditionally identified as an apple, the fruit that Eve and Adam eat is never defined. It could have been a banana for all we know.

Exit from Egypt

What is it?

It's an escape story. The title of the book means "Exit". (It comes from the Greek title *Exodos Aigyptou* which means "departure from Egypt".) Moses leads his oppressed people out of Egypt to freedom. It's action-packed, but it also contains the giving of the Law and instructions for worship.

Starring: Moses, Miriam, Pharaoh, Pharaoh's daughter, Aaron, and Joshua

@ EXODUS

This way out. With the Israelites enslaved in Egypt, God sends Moses to the rescue. Out in the desert, God gives the Law. But the people still worship idols.

IN TEN

1. Slavery: 1:1–14
2. Moses: 1:15 – 2:25
3. Burning bush: 3:1–21
4. Moses vs Pharaoh: 5:1–21
5. Plagues: 7:14 – 11:10
6. Passover: 12:1–42
7. Over the sea: 14:1–31
8. Manna: 16:1–26
9. Ten Commandments: 19:16 – 20:17
10. The golden calf: 32:1–35

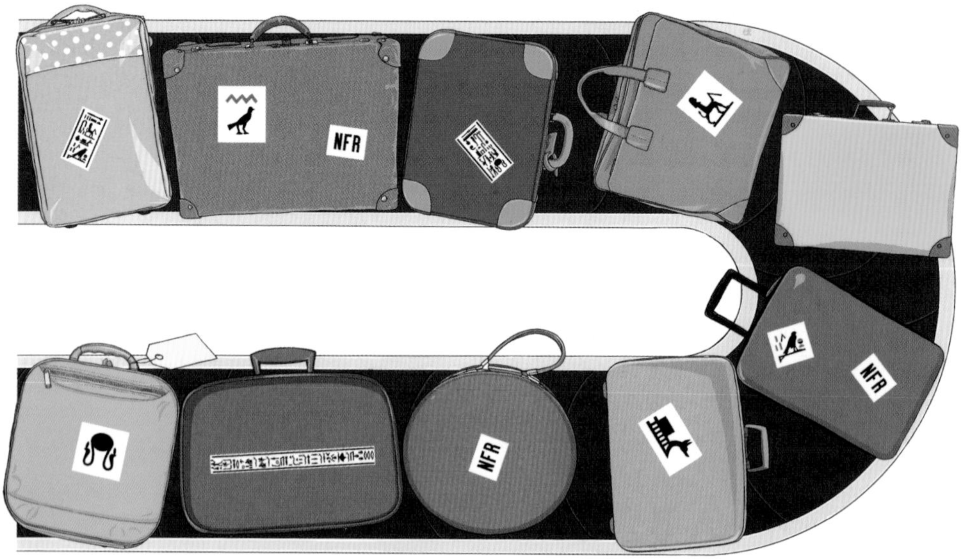

What happens?

Exodus starts in Egypt, where the Israelites have become slaves ❶. To curb the Israelite population, Pharaoh has instructed that every Hebrew baby boy is to be killed. But one mother takes her baby, puts him into a basket and sets him afloat to take his chances on the Nile. He is rescued by Pharaoh's daughter, who raises him as her own. She calls him Moses.

When he grows up, he sees an Egyptian master beating a Hebrew slave. Angry, he kills the bully, but the crime is discovered so he has to flee into the desert ❷. There, working as a shepherd, he sees a bush, which appears to be on fire but remains whole. God calls to Moses from within the fire and gives him the task of rescuing his people ❸. Moses returns to Egypt and confronts Pharaoh, who refuses to free the slaves ❹. So God inflicts a series of plagues on the Egyptians ❺. Still Pharaoh resists, so God sends one final, terrible plague: at midnight the angel of death will pass over the land, and the eldest sons of the Egyptians will die (and the eldest offspring of their livestock as well) ❻. Pharaoh relents and Moses leads the Israelites to freedom. But then Pharaoh sends chariots after them. Moses leads his people safely across the sea, but the pursuing chariots are drowned ❼.

In the desert, God provides food for his people in the form of quail and manna ❽. Three months after leaving Egypt, they come to Mount Sinai, where God gives Moses the Law by which he wants the Israelites to live ❾. At the bottom of the mountain the people worry that Moses isn't coming back, so they persuade Aaron to cast them a golden calf that they can worship. Moses rushes down the mountain, smashes the stone tablets on which God has inscribed the Law, and destroys the golden calf ❿. God gives Moses two new tablets, which he places in the ark of the covenant.

Why does it matter?

Exodus tells the story of how a group of escaping slaves become the people of God. This "rescue" becomes a core Bible theme. God also makes a covenant with them. Because he has rescued them, they agree to follow him and obey his laws.

Exodus includes some passages that still influence our lives today. Around the world, many legal systems are based on the Ten Commandments; millions of Jews still celebrate Passover.

The book also gives us a unique insight into God's character: he cares for his people, rescues them, and shows them how best to live. And he reveals to Moses his name: Yahweh, or "I am".

Surprise me !

The Hebrew title of the book, *Shemot*, is an abbreviation of "These are the names", which is the first line of the book.

The holiness manual

What is it?

Leviticus is named after the tribe of the Levites, which supplied all the priests for Israel (although they appear in only two verses in the book: Leviticus 25:32–34). This is essentially their priestly handbook, containing the rules and rituals that they and the people were to follow. Some ancient rabbis called the book *torat kohanim*: the manual of the priests.

Starring: Moses, Aaron, Nadab and Abihu, and introducing the Levites as the priests

@ LEVITICUS

"How to be holy" for beginners. A manual of religious and ethical behaviour for both the priests and the people.

IN FIVE

1. The priests are ordained: 8:1–36
2. The first sacrifice: 9:1–24
3. Clean and unclean animals: 11:1–47
4. The festivals: 23:1–44
5. The Jubilee: 25:1–55

What happens?

As regards a story, not much. There is hardly any "action" in the book. Aaron is ordained as the high priest ❶, the first sacrifice is offered ❷, and some priests disobey, with unfortunate consequences. That's about it for the action. The rest is a mass of rules and regulations telling the Israelites how to be holy. There is a long list of clean and unclean animals, for example – all the foods that Jews may or may not eat ❸. There are regulations covering everything from sacrifice to skin diseases, from criminal justice to clothing manufacture, from health and safety to holiness.

In some ways this is one of the least approachable books of the Bible. At times it is baffling, strange, and even unpleasant. For example, there is an emphasis on physical perfection which means that no one with any blemish can serve at the tabernacle: according to Leviticus, sores, burns, skin diseases, and even a woman's monthly period are enough to make a person unclean and force them to leave the camp. In this respect, Leviticus was part of the culture of its time. It was written for

a nomadic, Bronze-Age society which believed that only the perfect was good enough for God: perfect sacrifices, perfect animals, perfect priests. But there are also instructions for celebrating the many Jewish festivals ❹. There are radical social laws to help the poor and the needy. And there is legislation about the Year of Jubilee, a revolutionary economic and political concept which was unparalleled among the cultures of its time ❺.

Surprise me

In the list of unclean animals, the bat is included as a bird (Leviticus 11:19).

Why does it matter?

While Christians believe that the rituals and sacrifices have been superseded by Jesus, that doesn't mean Leviticus is redundant. It contains important principles about behaviour. It outlines the importance of sabbath. The festivals it describes are still celebrated by millions of Jews today (and form the background to Christian festivals such as Easter and Pentecost). And the Jubilee was a core image for Jesus – even today it is used to challenge financial and social injustice around the world.

The wilderness years

What is it?

It's a travel book. The title of the book comes from the census lists of people in each tribe – but they occupy only a small part of the book (two chapters: 1 and 26). The book really tells the story of a journey, one which takes the Israelites from Sinai to the borders of Canaan.

@ **NUMBERS**

God promises a land for his people. But getting there seems to be too tough for them. After forty years in the wilderness, a new generation prepares for the task.

What happens?

Numbers begins with the Jewish people preparing for their journey. Moses starts by taking a census of the travelling Israelites to see how many men are available to fight. There then follows some more stuff about the Law, including the special instructions for the Nazirites ❶. It is now one year since they left Egypt, and the Israelites celebrate the second Passover.

The second part of the book depicts the Israelites leaving Sinai, led by the ark of the covenant ❷, but it is not long before they start grumbling ❸. Even his own family is jealous of Moses ❹. When they reach the borders of Canaan, spies go in to scout out the land ❺. But, of the twelve spies sent in, ten declare victory impossible. Fearful, the people refuse to obey God. In return he sentences them to spend forty years in the wilderness ❻. The final section of the book describes their subsequent experiences. There is disobedience and rebellion ❼ – even Moses disobeys God's instructions ❽. Eventually they march again towards Canaan. After seeing their victories, the Moabite King Balak tries to use his prophet Balaam to curse the Israelites, but the plan

☆

Starring: Moses, Aaron, Miriam, Joshua, Caleb, Eleazar, Korah, and Balaam

Why does it matter?

Numbers continues the story of the exodus. Yes, it has some laws and all those names, but it's also got adventure, espionage, backbiting, plagues, and battles. Oh, and it's got a talking donkey. What more do you want?

is foiled by angelic intervention ❾. However, the Israelites intermarry with the Moabites and give in to the temptation to worship their god, Baal. As a result of this a plague hits them and 24,000 people die. After that there is a second census, and Joshua takes over the leadership of Israel from Moses (whose disobedience means that even he will not enter the land) ❿. The book ends with Israel at the border of Canaan, preparing to complete the task that should have been done forty years before.

IN TEN

10

❶ The Nazirites: 6:1–21
❷ Setting off: 10:11–35
❸ Complaints: 11:1–35
❹ Jealousy in Moses' family: 12:1–15
❺ The twelve spies: 13:1–33
❻ The punishment of the Israelites: 14:1–45
❼ Korah's rebellion: 16:1 – 17:13
❽ Moses' disobedience: 20:1–13
❾ Balaam's donkey: 22:1 – 23:12
❿ Joshua takes over: 27:12–23

Surprise me

The Hebrew title of the book is *bemidbar* – meaning "In the wilderness"– which as a title is a lot more exciting.

One more thing, before I go...

DEUTERONOMY

Moses reminds the people of what God has done and prepares them to enter the land. But he won't be there: this is his big goodbye.

What is it?

It's a farewell speech. Think of a retirement party, or the Oscars. Only much, much longer. At the end of his life, Moses reminds the people of all that God has done for them and the laws that he has given them to live by. Indeed, the name "Deuteronomy" means "repetition of the law".

Starring: Moses and Joshua

IN TEN

1. Starting over: 1:1–46
2. Take care: 4:1–14
3. Ten Commandments: 5:1–33
4. Love the Lord your God: 6:1–25
5. Ark and tablets: 10:1–9
6. Offerings: 26:1–19
7. Blessings: 28:1–14
8. Joshua: 31:1–8
9. Moses' song: 31:30 – 32:47
10. Moses' death: 34:1–12

What happens?

Deuteronomy begins with Moses and the people in Moab, just where the Jordan flows into the Dead Sea. Moses, realizing he isn't going to go with them, gives a series of farewell speeches to the people he has led. In the first section, he retells events from their history, such as the exodus and the wandering in the wilderness ❶. He then urges them to remember and obey the laws of God ❷.

There then follows a lengthy restatement of the Law, including the Ten Commandments ❸ and the most important commandment ❹. Moses explains the way to live as God's chosen nation and the regulations about the ark of the covenant and the tabernacle ❺. He issues promises of blessings if Israel obeys God, and dire warnings of the consequences should they disobey. He urges Israel to reject idolatry and to obey the rules on tithes and offerings ❻, and warns them of what will happen if they fail to do so ❼. These warnings look far ahead, to a time when the Israelites will be in exile and when all the dreams of a Promised Land will seem to have turned to dust. The Lord warns of punishment, but he also promises that he will bring his people back (30:1–10). In chapters 31 through to 34, there is a restatement of the handover of leadership from Moses to Joshua ❽. Moses blesses the tribes – a reminder of Jacob blessing his sons almost 450 years earlier in Egypt ❾. Finally, God shows Moses the Promised Land, although he cannot enter it, and Moses dies on Mount Nebo ❿.

Why does it matter?

More than any other book of the Bible, Deuteronomy forms the basis of Judaism – both at the time of Jesus and ever since. Many Jewish objects, such as the *tefillin* (small boxes containing verses from the Torah, worn by observant Jews during prayers) and the *tzitzit* (a fringed prayer garment), originate in Deuteronomy, as does Judaism's most famous prayer – the *Shema* (6:4–9) – and what is probably their most ancient creed (26:5–10). But Deuteronomy is more than just rules and regulations. The God reflected by Deuteronomy is caring and personal. He teaches his people, feeds them, and clothes them. And finally he leads them to a home of their own.

Surprise me !

The New Testament values Deuteronomy highly. It contains nearly one hundred quotations from it.

March to victory

What is it?

A war movie. And a gory one at that. The book takes its name from its hero, Joshua, son of Nun, successor to Moses, a veteran campaigner who is now eighty years old. It tells how the Israelites finally cross the Jordan and conquer Canaan, the land that God has given them.

Surprise me !

The Canaanite prostitute Rahab was the mother of Boaz, and the great-great-grandmother of King David. She actually turns up in the family tree of Jesus (Matthew 1:5).

@ JOSHUA

Miraculous victories as the Israelites conquer the land of Canaan. "Kill them all" is the instruction, but it's not as easy as that.

IN TEN (10)

- ❶ Be strong: 1:1–9
- ❷ Rahab: 2:1–24
- ❸ River crossing: 3:14 – 4:9
- ❹ The fall of Jericho: 6:1–27
- ❺ Achan: 7:1–26
- ❻ Hailstones: 10:1–11
- ❼ Occupation: 10:40–43; 11:12–20
- ❽ Allocating the land: 13:1–7
- ❾ Safe towns: 20:1–9
- ❿ Final challenge: 24:11–28

What happens?

The book begins with God telling Joshua to make preparations for the invasion ❶. He sends two spies into Jericho, who are protected by a prostitute called Rahab ❷. After this they cross the Jordan – and the flood-swollen river is miraculously held back by the power of God ❸.

After they have entered the land, they set about conquering city-state after city-state, starting with the miraculous collapse of the walls of Jericho ❹. At Ai, Achan disobeys instructions and keeps some plunder, and disaster follows ❺. When they obey God, success follows, and on their second attempt the city falls. At the battle at Gibeon, the Amorites are hailstoned to death! ❻ From there, the Israelites occupy the south and then the north, until finally there is peace ❼. Each tribe is allocated territory in which to live ❽, with the exception of

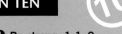

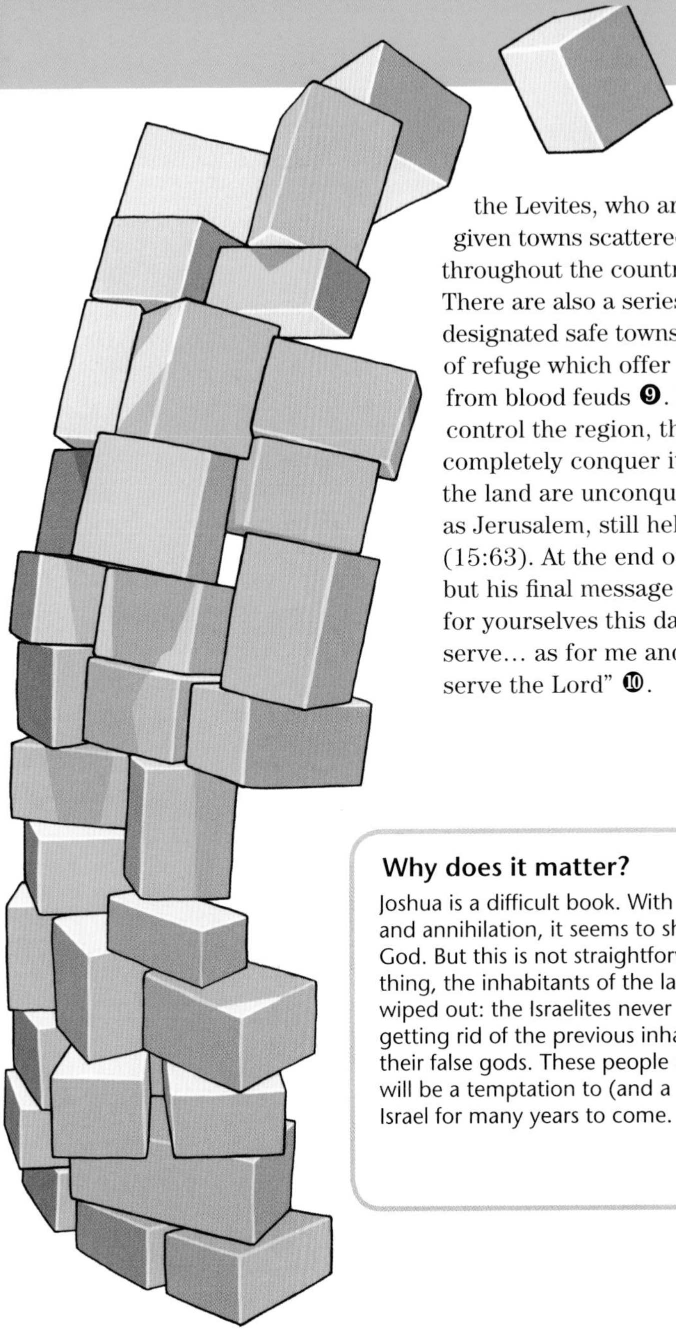

Starring: Joshua, Caleb, Rahab, Achan, Phinehas, and Eleazar

the Levites, who are given towns scattered throughout the country. There are also a series of designated safe towns – places of refuge which offer protection for fugitives from blood feuds ❾. But, although they control the region, the Israelites never do completely conquer it. Scattered throughout the land are unconquered cities such as Jerusalem, still held by the Jebusites (15:63). At the end of all this, Joshua dies, but his final message is a challenge: "Choose for yourselves this day whom you will serve… as for me and my household, we will serve the Lord" ❿.

Why does it matter?

Joshua is a difficult book. With its depictions of conquest and annihilation, it seems to show a vengeful, violent God. But this is not straightforward history. For one thing, the inhabitants of the land are not completely wiped out: the Israelites never complete the job of getting rid of the previous inhabitants and removing their false gods. These people and the gods they worship will be a temptation to (and a cause of the downfall of) Israel for many years to come.

Every man for himself

What is it?

A horror movie. This is undoubtedly the goriest book of the Bible. From the rule of Joshua to the establishment of the monarchy, this is a time of anarchy, typified by the repeated phrase "In those days Israel had no king; everyone did as he saw fit" (21:25). It shows a grim repeating pattern: the people turn away from God; God sends a foreign nation to punish them; the people cry out to God for deliverance; God sends them a "judge" to deliver them. Then the people turn away again...

@ **JUDGES**

Instructions:
1. Worship idols so you are oppressed by enemies. 2. Call on God to help. 3. He sends a judge to the rescue. Pause, and then repeat.

☆ **Starring: Othniel, Ehud, Eglon, Deborah, Gideon, Abimelech, Jephthah, Samson, and Delilah**

What happens?

Judges starts with a captured king having his thumbs and big toes cut off, and goes downhill from there. The problem is that Israel never did conquer all the land ❶. The people of Israel keep abandoning the God who has led them to safety and turning, time and time again, to other gods ❷.

We get Eglon, King of Moab, who is assassinated by Ehud the left-handed assassin ❸; we see the army of Jabin of Canaan, which is defeated by Deborah and her general, Barak ❹. Typically for Judges, the enemy general, Sisera, is killed by having a tent peg driven through his head. This inspires one of the oldest passages in the Bible – the song of Deborah ❺.

After this, the Midianites are the oppressors, and God calls Gideon to fight them ❻. In order to prove it is God's doing, Gideon reduces his fighting force to just 300 men, but still sends the Midianites packing ❼. After the Midianites come the Philistines – and their big enemy is Samson. Set apart at birth ❽, Samson is a man of prodigious strength ❾ but he is undermined by his taste for foreign women. Captured by the Philistines, he is displayed as a captive at one of their feasts. He pushes apart the pillars holding up the roof, killing himself and all the Philistines in the Temple. (Technically, he's the world's first suicide bomber.) ❿

IN TEN

❶ **Unfinished task: 1:27–35**

❷ **Israel is punished: 2:6–19**

❸ **Ehud and Eglon: 3:12–30**

❹ **Deborah and Barak: 4:1–24**

❺ **Deborah's song: 5:1–31**

❻ **Gideon is chosen: 6:11–40**

❼ **The army is chosen: 7:1–25**

❽ **Samson's birth: 13:1–25**

❾ **Samson's strength: 15:1–20**

❿ **Samson and Delilah: 16:4–31**

Why does it matter?

Judges is a grim, violent book. But that's the point. It's a picture of what happens to a society when it abandons God, when everyone lives for themselves. Even the judges themselves are morally ambivalent: they frequently start well and end up just as bad as everyone else. But that means that Judges, in some ways, is a strikingly modern book. It's horrible, but it's the kind of horror that can be found today in many war zones and areas of urban deprivation.

Surprise me

The book is named after the leaders God chose to rescue Israel: the "judges" were a mix of lawmakers and tribal chieftains, who not only fought battles but decided legal cases and even performed religious rituals.

Love and redemption

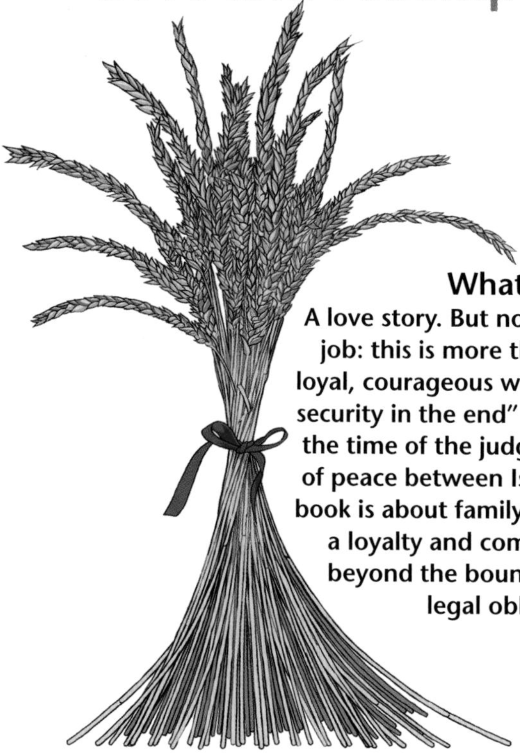

What is it?

A love story. But not a soppy, romantic job: this is more the "hard-working, loyal, courageous woman finds love and security in the end" kind of thing. Set in the time of the judges, during a period of peace between Israel and Moab, the book is about family duty, affection, and a loyalty and commitment that go beyond the boundaries of duty or legal obligation.

@ RUTH

Ruth to Naomi: your God is my God. They return to Bethlehem, where Boaz notices Ruth's faithfulness. Ruth ♥ Boaz.

What happens?

Naomi is an Israelite woman living in Moab. Her husband has died, as have her two sons, so she decides to return to her home town of Bethlehem alone ❶.

However, one of her daughters-in-law, Ruth (who is a Moabitess), insists on staying with her and adopting Naomi's God as her own ❷. "Don't urge me to leave you or to turn back from you," she says. "Where you go I will go, and where you stay I will stay. Your people will be my people, and your God my God" (1:16).

Starring: Ruth, Naomi, and Boaz

They return to Bethlehem and Ruth goes to follow the barley harvest, hoping to pick up the grain dropped by the men as they reap. (The Torah instructed that, during the harvest, any stalks that were dropped must be left for the poor.) The field that Ruth chooses belongs to a man called Boaz, who finds out about Ruth's loyalty and not only allows Ruth to glean but also gives her protection and even leaves extra grain for her ❸.

This gives Naomi an idea, and she encourages Ruth to seek marriage with Boaz as a kinsman-redeemer. In the society of the time, the nearest kin is obliged to "redeem" a widow – to marry her so that the dead husband would have an heir and the woman would have security. Naomi gets Ruth to go that night to the threshing floor where Boaz is working, and "uncover his feet" while he is sleeping. When Boaz asks who is there she spreads out her cloak, which is probably a symbolic way of asking for marriage. Boaz is impressed by her loyalty, and decides that he will redeem her ❹. But there's a problem: technically, he's not the nearest relative. So he goes to the gate of the city and finds that relative, and persuades him to forego his rights. Ruth marries Boaz and they have a son, Obed. And he is the grandfather of King David ❺.

IN FIVE 5

- ❶ **Deaths in the family: 1:1–7**
- ❷ **Ruth's choice: 1:8–22**
- ❸ **Ruth meets Boaz: 2:1–23**
- ❹ **Naomi's plan: 3:1–18**
- ❺ **Ruth and Boaz are married: 4:1–22**

Surprise me !

In the Hebrew text the other male relative is called "Ploni Almoni", which is a joke name: it means so-and-so, Joe Bloggs, or Joe Schmo.

Why does it matter?

Ruth is a wonderful story in itself, but its importance lies in its heroine. The person who most embodies selfless love in this book is not an Israelite but Ruth from Moab, a despised and hated enemy of Israel. She demonstrates that participation in the kingdom of God is nothing to do with nationality, but rather a matter of loving God and following his commands. Ruth is so honoured that this foreign woman finds a mention in the family tree of Christ (Matthew 1:5).

We want a king!

What is it?

History and intense psychological drama. The book is a history of Israel from the close of the time of the judges to the establishment of the kingdom under David. It shows the rise to power of the first two kings of Israel, Saul and his rival, David.

@ **1SAMUEL**
Israel wants a king. God tells Samuel 2 anoint Saul, but then chooses David. D kills Goliath; Saul goes mad. D flees; Saul dies in battle.

IN TEN

❶ Samuel's calling: 3:1–21
❷ The capture of the ark: 4:1 – 5:12
❸ We want a king: 8:1–22
❹ Saul is king: 10:1–27
❺ David is chosen: 15:34 – 16:13
❻ David vs Goliath: 17:1–58
❼ Saul vs David: 19:1–18
❽ David lets Saul live: 24:1–22
❾ Saul talks to a ghost: 28:1–25
❿ Saul dies: 31:1–13

What happens?

Born as a result of prayer, Samuel is dedicated to God from birth, and brought up at the shrine containing the tabernacle ❶. Israel is in turmoil. At one stage the Philistines capture the ark of the covenant, but it brings plagues, so they send it back ❷. The people ask Samuel to appoint a king. Samuel tells them that God is against the idea, but they insist ❸. God leads Samuel to Saul, a boy from the tribe of Benjamin, who becomes the first king of Israel ❹.

Saul defeats the Ammonites and has the Spirit of God on him. But he is headstrong, impatient, and disobedient. In the end, the Lord rejects Saul. Samuel finds the next king in Bethlehem. The youngest son of Jesse (and great-grandson of Ruth and Boaz), David is a shepherd, musician, and poet – and a fierce warrior ❺. The Philistines invade again, this time with their champion, a giant called Goliath. David is the only one who is willing to take on Goliath and, using a sling and a rock, he kills the giant ❻. The Philistines flee and David becomes a hero.

David's popularity maddens Saul. He plans to kill David, even though he is

Starring: Eli, Hannah, Samuel, Saul, Jonathan, David, and Michal

now married to his daughter and is close friends with his son Jonathan. When Jonathan warns David that his life is in danger, David flees ❼. He becomes a guerrilla, hiding in caves. Twice he has the opportunity to kill Saul, but he refuses ❽.

The Philistines invade *again*. Saul goes to a witch, who conjures up the spirit of (the now-deceased) Samuel, who tells Saul he is doomed ❾. On Mount Gilboa, Saul and Jonathan are defeated and Saul takes his own life. The Philistines find the bodies of Saul and his sons, cut off their heads, and fasten their bodies to the walls of Beth Shan ❿.

Surprise me !

When the Philistines capture the ark, they are struck by plagues involving mice and "tumours". Some scholars think the latter is bubonic plague. Others think that the Hebrew word actually means hemorrhoids. Ouch.

Why does it matter?

1 Samuel is an important slice of history. It introduces us to some key figures: Samuel, the first prophet, Saul, the failure as a king, and, of course, David, the founder of the line of kings that will lead, in the end, to Jesus.

Simply... **2 SAMUEL**

Rise and fall

@ 2SAMUEL
Going up: David defeats enemies, unites the kingdom. Going down: D gets woman pregnant; kills husband. Son rebels. D sins but also repents.

What is it?

Soap opera: Middle-Eastenders. The second half of the book of Samuel tells the story of the rise and fall of King David. It is the story of how Israel's greatest king gains control of the kingdom, only to lose control of himself and his family.

What happens?

After Saul's death, there are seven years of civil war. At Hebron, David is anointed king over Judah in the south, while Saul's son Ish-Bosheth is supported by the tribes of Israel in the north ❶. Eventually, Ish-Bosheth is assassinated and David unites the kingdom ❷. David goes on to defeat Israel's enemies. He captures Jerusalem, makes it his new capital, and brings the ark of the covenant into the city ❸. God makes a covenant with him: the house of David will rule for ever ❹.

And then it all goes wrong. David commits adultery with Bathsheba, wife of his general, Uriah. When she becomes pregnant, David arranges for Uriah's death in battle ❺. But the crime does not go undetected. He is confronted by the prophet Nathan, who tells him that, because of his sin, Bathsheba's baby will

Starring: David, Joab, Bathsheba, Nathan, and Absalom

die and conflict will always be a part of his family and household ❻.

Nathan's prediction proves true. The baby dies and, in time, Bathsheba has another son, whom they call Solomon. But David's family is dysfunctional in the extreme. One of his sons rapes one of his daughters ❼. Another son, Absalom, attempts a coup against his father ❽. David escapes from Jerusalem and his forces defeat Absalom's army near the Forest of Ephraim. Absalom tries to escape, but his head gets caught in the thick branches of an oak tree and he is murdered as he hangs there ❾. Finally, David angers God by conducting a census and a plague strikes the land ❿.

Why does it matter?

King David. The greatest king of Israel. The golden boy. Yet he had feet of clay. That's why 2 Samuel matters. Because it shows that David's "greatness" lay not in his military success, not even in his rule as king, but in his response to God. Faced with personal failure and sin, he throws himself on God's mercy. What makes David special is not his ability to rule, but his willingness to repent.

IN TEN

10

- ❶ King David of Judah, King Ish-Bosheth of Israel: 2:1–11
- ❷ Ish-Bosheth assassinated: 4:1–12
- ❸ The conquest of Jerusalem: 5:1–12; 6:1–23
- ❹ God's promise: 7:1–29
- ❺ David and Bathsheba: 11:1–27
- ❻ Nathan accuses the king: 12:1–23
- ❼ The rape of Tamar: 13:1–39
- ❽ Absalom rebels: 15:1–31
- ❾ Absalom is killed: 18:1–33
- ❿ David's final sin: 24:1–25

Surprise me !

1 & 2 Samuel is actually one book. It was split into two because the whole thing would not fit on one scroll.

Glory and shame

What is it?

It's a history lesson. A documentary, taking us from the death of David through the reign of Solomon and on to the splitting of the kingdom into two separate nations, with their many kings and rulers. In each case, the author decides whether they are a good king or a bad king. Each one is measured according to whether he obeys the commands of the Lord. Mostly, they choose disobedience.

IN TEN

1. The death of David: 1:1 – 2:12
2. Solomon's wisdom: 3:1–28
3. The building of the Temple: 5:1 – 6:14
4. The dedication of the Temple: 8:1–66
5. Solomon's stupidity: 11:1–13, 41–43
6. The splitting of the kingdom: 12:1–20
7. Jeroboam and the golden calves: 12:25–33
8. Enter Elijah: 17:1–24
9. Elijah vs Baal: 18:1–46
10. The Lord appears to Elijah: 19:1–21

Starring: David, Solomon, Rehoboam, Jeroboam, Elijah, Ahab, and Jezebel

What happens?

Kings begins with the death of David ❶. He is succeeded – after some violence – by Solomon, who is famous for his God-given wisdom ❷. Solomon builds a magnificent Temple in Jerusalem ❸. When the ark is brought into it, the glory of the Lord descends ❹.

But Solomon crashes to the ground. His hundreds of pagan wives lure him into worshipping foreign gods ❺. And during the building of the Temple he inflicts heavier taxes on the northern tribes. When he dies, these tribes ask Solomon's son Rehoboam to lighten their load, but he refuses. So they rebel. Ten tribes became the northern kingdom of Israel, while the two tribes of Judah and Benjamin form the southern kingdom of Judah. Rehoboam rules Judah, and Israel appoints Jeroboam as its new king ❻.

Israel starts badly. Jeroboam creates a new religion and builds two idols for the people to worship ❼. In the meantime Rehoboam also starts to worship other Gods. And that's how it continues. Of all the kings listed in 1 Kings, only two are good: Asa and Jehoshaphat. The rest are downright evil.

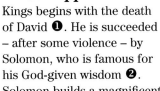

Among the worst are King Ahab of Israel and his Phoenician wife, Jezebel, who introduce the worship of Baal God sends the prophet Elijah to counter them ❽. In a climactic battle at Mount Carmel Elijah defeats the prophets of Baal ❾. After this he flees into the desert, where God meets with him at Mount Sinai. He returns and appoints his successor, Elisha ❿. The book ends with the death of Ahab in Israel, and the successful reign of Jehoshaphat in Judah.

@ 1KINGS

Solomon builds the Temple but breaks the kingdom. It splits into Israel & Judah. Many bad kings. God sends a prophetic warning (Elijah).

Why does it matter?

Kings is important for the rise of the prophets. God almost washes his hands of the rulers of the kingdoms, and instead speaks through his prophets. From now on it will be these people who hold the powers to account. We find in Kings this important underlying principle: it's not enough to be rich and powerful; you have to obey God.

Surprise me !

According to the Bible, Solomon had 700 wives and 300 concubines. It doesn't say whether he remembered all their birthdays.

Decline and fall

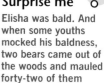

Surprise me !

Elisha was bald. And when some youths mocked his baldness, two bears came out of the woods and mauled forty-two of them (2:23–24).

What is it?

Tragedy. On an epic scale. The second book of Kings carries on the story of 1 Kings and we see the not-so-good ships Israel and Judah sail into a perfect storm of idolatrous kings, disobedient people, and malevolent superpowers.

@ 2KINGS

Bad kings lead people astray. Israel destroyed by Assyrians; 150 years later, Judah exiled by Babylonians. All predicted by prophets.

What happens?

2 Kings begins with the departure of Elijah ❶. His successor is Elisha, who carries out many miracles including healing a man from leprosy ❷ and even single-handedly defeating the Syrian army ❸. God even instructs Elisha to "appoint" a new king of Syria ❹, and one of his "assistant" prophets anoints Jehu king over Israel. Jehu kills Joram, son of Ahab, and the Queen Mother, Jezebel ❺.

Ahab and Jezebel's daughter, Athaliah, has married one of the kings of Judah. When her son dies, she seizes the throne and tries to annihilate the house of David by killing all her grandchildren. But one survives – Joash, who is hidden in the Temple. Seven years later he is brought out of hiding and returned to the throne and his evil granny is killed. The house of David survives ❻.

Starring: Elijah, Elisha, Naaman, Jezebel, Jehu, Athaliah, Joash, Hezekiah, Isaiah, Manasseh and Josiah, and introducing the Assyrians and the Babylonians.

The events of 2 Kings form the background to the writings of prophets such as Isaiah, Jeremiah, Ezekiel, Amos, and Hosea. And what they predict all the time is the demise of the kingdoms at the hands of their enemies.

Israel goes first. In 722 BC, after many years of threats, the Assyrian empire invades. The kingdom is destroyed and all the people are taken into captivity. The ten tribes of Israel disappear off the map ❼.

Judah, the southern kingdom, staggers on for another 150 years or so. It even manages some good kings in the form of Hezekiah ❽ and Josiah ❾. But it too fails to worship God, and in 586 BC the Babylonians invade. The Temple is destroyed and the majority of the population taken away to Babylon ❿.

IN TEN

❶ Elijah departs: 2:1–18
❷ Naaman: 5:1–27
❸ Elisha vs the Syrian army: 6:8–23
❹ The tears of a prophet: 8:7–15
❺ The death of Jezebel: 9:1–37
❻ Athaliah and Joash: 11:1–21
❼ Destruction of Israel: 17:1–23
❽ Hezekiah: 18:1–4; 19:1–37
❾ King Josiah and the Law: 22:1–20; 23:21–23
❿ The destruction of Jerusalem: 25:1–30

Why does it matter?

2 Kings shows that God is in charge. It reveals how the invading kingdoms are tools for God's judgment. Those who wrote and compiled Kings were probably in exile in Babylon. And they were there not by chance, but because the exile was a punishment brought about by their continued disobedience to God.

And now for the highlights...

What is it?

It's an official portrait of the king with hefty airbrushing. It's a Photoshopped® version of 2 Samuel, with all the blemishes removed. It's not really interested in Israel, because Israel has gone. Chronicles concerns itself with Judah. Similarly, the picture of David has been manipulated: in 1 Chronicles, he is given the full-on hero treatment. There is no mention of the seven-year civil war, and nothing at all about Bathsheba.

@ **1CHRONICLES**
David becomes king, captures Jerusalem, plans the Temple and dies a happy death. This is history as written by the priests.

IN FIVE

❶ **David becomes king: 11:1–9**
❷ **The joyful return of the ark: 15:1–29**
❸ **"Your descendants will be kings": 17:1–26**
❹ **Building plot: 21:1 – 22:1**
❺ **Last words: 29:1–30**

What happens?

The book starts with lengthy genealogies which emphasize the continuation of the house of David and the connection with the ongoing story of the Jews, right back to Genesis. After that, it's into the life of David. Details about Saul's reign are limited to his death. We then skip the civil war and move straight to David's coronation and capture of Jerusalem ❶. There is a lot of material about the transportation of the ark, its installation in the capital ❷, and the ceremonies that went with that. God makes a covenant with David that his house will last for ever ❸. Then we have a list of the military victories of David, and the only glitch in the book: the "sinful" census, which is punished by a plague. As penance for the plague, David buys the site on which to build the Temple ❹. Then we have a detailed account of the plans for the Temple, covering not only its construction but also the staffing and organization. The book ends with David's death, his final thanksgiving prayer, and the accession of Solomon ❺.

Starring: David

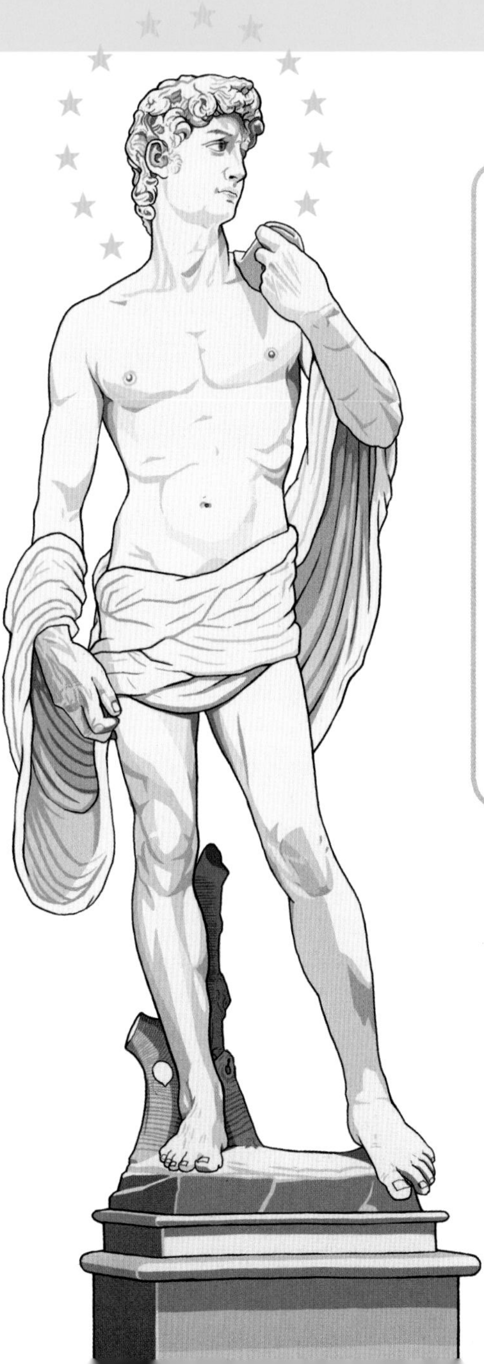

Why does it matter?

Chronicles is not history as we know it – there is too much missing. This book comes from a definitely religious perspective. It is not interested in the Jews as a political or military entity, but as a worshipping community. And it aims to answer a simple question: "Does God care about his people any more?"

After the shattering experience of exile in Babylon, Chronicles retells their history to show that the Judah that was re-established after the exile was a continuation of the past. In particular, David – the person who made Jerusalem great, who planned the Temple and who brought the ark of the covenant into the city – is powerful because he trusts in the Lord.

Surprise me

The name "Chronicles" comes not from the Hebrew but from Jerome's Latin translation (AD 385–405), which calls the book *Chronicorum Liber*.

The highlights, part two

What is it?

Sometimes when a sports team loses a fixture, the manager says that they have to take positives out of it. That's what 2 Chronicles is. It's the story of the decline and fall of Israel, but with a positive spin. Written for those Jews returning to Judah after the exile, 2 Chronicles focuses on those kings who choose to live godly lives, giving extensive treatment to good, reforming kings such as Hezekiah, Jehoshaphat, Joash, and Asa. But perhaps the main character in the book is not a human at all, but the Temple itself. This is a book in which the worship of God is central. And 2 Chronicles pretty much ignores the (now defunct) northern kingdom of Israel because of that kingdom's idolatry and refusal to acknowledge the Temple in Jerusalem.

Starring: Solomon, Rehoboam, Jeroboam, Uzziah, Hezekiah, and Josiah, and featuring The Temple as itself

2CHRONICLES
In this version of history, the kings who do well are those who make the worship of God central. Important message for the returning exiles.

What happens?

Solomon accedes to the throne, ushering in a golden age of prosperity and peace ❶. His wisdom becomes legendary, and, most importantly, he builds the Temple ❷. (Six out of the nine "Solomon" chapters

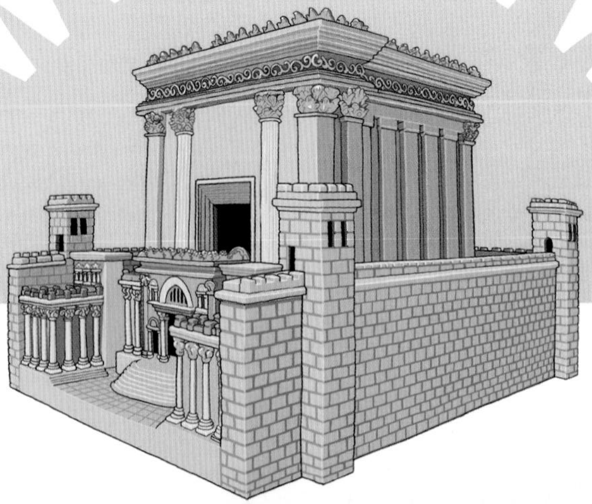

are concerned with the construction and dedication of this building.) Sadly, this glory is short-lived. After Solomon's death the kingdom splits in two. 2 Chronicles then focuses on the southern kingdom – Judah – and its twenty rulers. It's not all black and white. Some of the bad kings are shown to have seen the error of their ways: Rehoboam humbles himself before God and averts his anger; Manasseh, who is irredeemably evil in Kings, is shown as repenting. And some of the good kings end badly. Asa conquers enemies against great odds, yet fails to trust God when threatened by Israel; Uzziah is blessed with military victories, but presumptuously takes on the role of a priest and is therefore stricken with leprosy ❸. There is Jehoshaphat, who brings in a great revival, Joash, who repairs the Temple and restores the worship of the Lord, and Hezekiah, who repairs and reopens the Temple, cleanses Judah from the idolatry of his wicked father, Ahaz, and is therefore spared destruction by Assyria ❹. Finally, Josiah reforms the kingdom, rediscovers the Law and holds the first "proper" Passover since the time of Samuel ❺. In the end, of course, disaster cannot be averted, and the Babylonians destroy the kingdom. But the message is clear: those who worship the Lord will be rewarded.

Why does it matter?

It may seem like partial, airbrushed history, but the message of 2 Chronicles is simple: "success" is about trusting in the Lord. Those kings who value the Temple and put the worship of the Lord at the heart of the nation are the "good" kings. 2 Chronicles is not so much a proper history as a call to repentance and pure worship. Addressed to Jews who have returned from the exile, it uses the history of their nation to show them what truly matters: the worship of God and obedience to the Law.

IN FIVE 5

- ❶ **Solomon's wealth: 1:1–17**
- ❷ **Solomon dedicates the Temple: 7:1–22**
- ❸ **Uzziah: 26:1–23**
- ❹ **Hezekiah vs Assyria: 32:1–30**
- ❺ **Josiah, the Law, and the Passover: 34:1–33; 35:1–19**

Surprise me !

According to tradition, Ezra is the author of Chronicles (not to mention of Ezra and Nehemiah). The author was probably a priest, who had access to a number of documents: Chronicles draws on several historical sources, including *The Books of the Kings of Judah and Israel* (2 Chronicles 28:26), *The Book of the Annals of King David* (1 Chronicles 27:24), *The Chronicles of Samuel the Seer*, *The Chronicles of Nathan the Prophet* and, *The Chronicles of Gad the Seer* (1 Chronicles 29:29).

Back to the future

What is it?

3 Chronicles. Well, probably, anyway; the beginning of Ezra is virtually identical to the end of Chronicles, so it's likely that Ezra is a continuation by the same author. The book tells the story of two returns home. The first sees Jews led by Zerubbabel return to Jerusalem and start rebuilding the Temple. The second half of the book deals with the return of Ezra. He stops the people from intermarrying with the tribes around them and calls them back to focus on God. The traditional view is that Ezra is the author of the book (some of which is written in the first person).

Starring: Ezra, Cyrus, Darius and Artaxerxes, Joshua, Zerubbabel, Nehemiah, Haggai, and Zechariah

What happens?

In 539 BC Cyrus of Persia overthrows the Babylonian empire and issues a decree that allows the captive Judeans to return to their homeland ❶. Relatively few committed individuals decide to accompany their leader, Zerubbabel, back to Judea. Zerubbabel begins by restoring the altar and reinstituting the sacrifices and then starts work on the Temple building itself. However, in the face of opposition from other inhabitants of the region, progress grinds to a halt ❷. The prophets Haggai and Zechariah exhort the people to return to work and it is finished by about 515 BC ❸.

The second section of Ezra takes place some eighty years after the first return, in 457 BC. Ezra the priest is given authority by Artaxerxes I to take a group of exiles back with contributions for the Temple ❹. Numbering fewer than 2,000 people (including many priests and Levites), they arrive safely in Jerusalem, but the situation there is depressing: the residents have intermarried with the surrounding peoples, leading to compromise and confusion. Ezra calls on them to put away their foreign wives and return to living in accordance with God's laws ❺.

Why does it matter?

Ezra is a story of restoration. But it is not just the restoration of the Temple: it is also about the spiritual and moral restoration of the people and, indeed, the restoration of hope and self-respect. It takes us forward in the story of God's faithfulness to his people in exile and the fulfilment of his promise delivered through his prophets: that the exiles would return and the city would be rebuilt.

@ EZRA

Zerubbabel leads the first Judeans back from exile. Later Ezra returns with another group and calls on the people to recommit themselves to God.

IN FIVE

❶ **Return: 1:1–11**
❷ **Rebuilding and opposition: 3:7 – 4:5**
❸ **Haggai gets them going again: 5:1 – 6:15**
❹ **Ezra returns: 7:1–27**
❺ **Confession and reparation: 10:1–17**

Surprise me !

Ezra was a really important figure in Judaism: he was the person who brought the Torah back from Babylon and read it out to the people (Nehemiah chapters 8–10).

Prayer and action

What is it?

4 Chronicles. Oh, all right, maybe not, but it does take the story of return on, and it is probable that the book was begun by the same person who compiled Chronicles and Ezra. It tells the story of the third return to Jerusalem, when a group of exiles under Nehemiah make their way back to their homeland. The work there has ground to a halt (again) and the city walls have not been repaired. Under the influence and inspiration of Nehemiah the walls are repaired in just fifty-two days.

@ **NEHEMIAH**
Things are bad in Jerusalem. Nehemiah returns to help repair the walls and restore the faith. He is a man of action and a man of prayer.

Starring: Nehemiah, Ezra and Artaxerxes, with Sanballat the Horonite, Tobiah the Ammonite, and Geshem the Arab as "the villains"

What happens?

The story opens in Susa, the capital of Persia. Nehemiah, a high-ranking Jewish official at the Persian king's palace, hears news from Jerusalem: the gates of the city have been burned and the walls destroyed. The holy city is at risk ❶. So Nehemiah takes steps. He approaches King Artaxerxes and obtains permission to return ❷. Artaxerxes even gives him some building supplies to take with him, and Nehemiah leads a group of exiles back.

Once in Jerusalem, Nehemiah inspects the

walls and starts the rebuilding ❸. But he faces threats and opposition from three local warlords: Sanballat the Horonite, Tobiah the Ammonite, and Geshem the Arab ❹. Inside the city there are problems as well: the richer Jews are oppressing the people, forcing them to sell their children and mortgage their property or else be taken into slavery ❺. Nehemiah combines prayer and action to deal with the threat. He leads by example, going without any form of salary. The walls are finished and dedicated in a remarkable fifty-two days ❻. The priest Ezra has a special wooden platform built where he sits and reads the Law to the people ❼. They respond with confession and prayer and with the celebration of the ancient Feast of Tabernacles or Booths (Jewish *Sukkot*) – the first time this festival has been celebrated since the time of the judges ❽.

Nehemiah returns to Susa. Later, he hears that things have slipped back ❾. He makes a final trip back to Jerusalem around 425 BC, when he cleanses the Temple and reinforces sabbath observation ❿.

IN TEN

- ❶ **Nehemiah's tears: 1:1–11**
- ❷ **A request: 2:1–10**
- ❸ **The walls: 2:11–20**
- ❹ **Opposition: 4:1–23**
- ❺ **Concern for the poor: 5:1–19**
- ❻ **Finishing the defences: 6:1–19**
- ❼ **Ezra reads the Law: 8:1–12**
- ❽ **Tabernacles: 8:13–18**
- ❾ **More news from Jerusalem: 13:1–9**
- ❿ **Return to the sabbath: 13:15–31**

Why does it matter?

Nehemiah is about prayer and action. Everything that Nehemiah does grows out of prayer and dedication to God. But, having prayed to God, or confessed their sins, the people have to act. This results in either rebuilding the physical walls of the city or rebuilding the spiritual walls of their faith. This book is not just about rebuilding Jerusalem; it's about restoring the faith, rebuilding the ancient festivals, and dedicating yourself to God.

Surprise me

When Ezra reads the Law to the people it has to be translated into Aramaic. By this time, after seventy years in exile, the people no longer speak Hebrew.

A time like this

Starring: Esther, Xerxes, Mordecai, and Haman

What is it?

It's a romantic adventure story, a fairy tale, with an evil villain and a beauty contest thrown in for good measure. Esther is a book about liberation and rescue. It shows how God works behind the scenes to rescue his people. This rescue is still celebrated today in the festival of Purim, which is described in the final chapter of the book.

What happens?

The scene opens in the winter palace of King Xerxes in Susa. He orders his beautiful queen, Vashti, to appear before him and be shown off at a lavish banquet. She refuses ❶. Furious, Xerxes deposes her and holds a beauty contest to find another wife. The winner is a young girl called Esther ❷. She is Jewish, but on the advice of her cousin, Mordecai, she hides that fact. With her help Mordecai is able to warn the king about an assassination plot, and his good deed is recorded in the official records ❸.

@ ESTHER

Esther wins the Xerxes-Factor and becomes queen. Haman plots to kill the Jews, but is himself killed when Esther reveals the truth.

Meanwhile, Haman, a high-ranking Persian official, insists that people should bow to him. Mordecai refuses and Haman plots his revenge. He manipulates Xerxes into signing a decree declaring that all Jews will be executed ❹. Desperate, Mordecai asks Esther to intercede on behalf of her countrymen. Esther starts to seek the right moment ❺.

One night, Xerxes cannot sleep and, to pass the time, he has the official records read to him. There he is reminded of Mordecai's deed, and decides to reward him. He summons Haman, who has already prepared for Mordecai's death ❻. Haman is deeply humiliated when he finds out that Mordecai is to be honoured ❼. At a banquet, Esther tells the king of her plight and reveals Haman's plot ❽. The king has Haman hanged on the very gallows that Haman had planned to use for Mordecai. Xerxes cannot rescind the order to attack the Jews, but he permits them to defend themselves, so they are saved ❾. The next day they hold a festival to celebrate their deliverance ❿.

IN TEN

10

❶ Vashti refuses to appear: 1:1–12

❷ Esther becomes queen: 2:1–18

❸ Mordecai saves the king: 2:19–23

❹ Haman's plot: 3:1–15

❺ Mordecai takes action: 4:1–17

❻ Haman builds the gallows: 5:1–14

❼ Xerxes honours Mordecai: 6:1–12

❽ Esther to the rescue: 7:1–10

❾ The Jews' defence: 8:1–17

❿ Purim: 9:20–32

Why does it matter?

Esther has become one of the most popular books among Jews, particularly because it is commemorated in the Jewish festival of Purim, a celebration of national deliverance. Esther reads like a fairy tale, but it has a serious side. It is about persecution and deliverance, and its message of perseverance and triumph has given strength to many Jews in similar circumstances down the centuries.

Surprise me !

Esther has one unusual feature: the book doesn't once mention God. This – and the fact that Esther marries a non-Jew – led to many rabbis having reservations about including the book in the final list of Hebrew scriptures.

Why me?

What is it?

A dark, brooding psychological drama. (Shot in black and white. Possibly with subtitles.) It's a meditation on one of the most profound of all human dilemmas: why do good people suffer? The book, set in the time of the patriarchs, takes the form of a dialogue or a debate between Job and various not-so-helpful friends.

@ JOB

This man has done nothing wrong. So why is he being punished? Justice for the Uz 1! #jobisinnocent

Starring: Job, Eliphaz, Bildad, Zophar, and Elihu. And introducing Leviathan as "the great big scary thing"

What happens?

Job is a genuinely good, God-fearing man. He lives in the land of Uz where he is blessed with riches, health and a big family. In heaven, God points to Job as a shining example of someone who fears God. In response, Satan – the accuser – claims that Job is only like that because he is so prosperous. So God gives Satan permission to attack: Job's family die and he loses all his wealth ❶. Even so, Job refuses to curse God. Satan argues that, if he loses his health, Job will *definitely* curse God. So God allows Satan to give Job a horrible disease. His suffering is too great for words ❷. Even so, he refuses to curse God. As he sits there, he is visited by three friends. Together they start to seek some kind of explanation for what has happened. Job wishes that he'd never been born ❸. His friends argue that he must have done something wrong, but Job rejects this. He hasn't sinned, and he wants an explanation ❹.

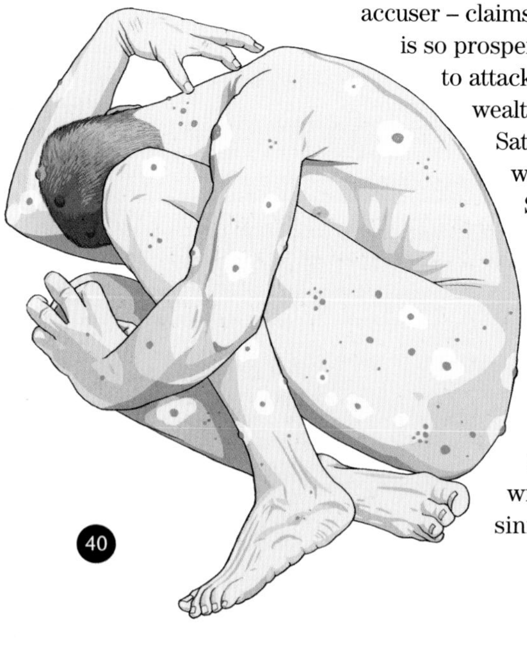

His friends continue to argue: he *must* have done something wrong. He should pray to God and seek his favour. He should repent. He's nothing but a sinner who talks a lot ❺. Job rejects all their arguments. He knows that he will be rescued in the end ❻. Finally, Job's three friends stop trying to argue with him. But then a new voice enters the debate: Elihu, a young man, who says that God is using suffering to purify Job's life ❼. Elihu's attempt to vindicate God is cut short. A whirlwind blows up and, out of the heart of this storm, God speaks. But rather than provide answers, he presents Job with a series of questions ❽. He is the mighty Lord, the only one powerful enough to tame Leviathan ❾. Job recognizes that he cannot comprehend the might of God. He puts his questions aside. His fortunes are restored and he dies an old man, who has lived a good, long life ❿.

IN TEN

❶ **Job loses everything: 1:1–22**
❷ **On the scrapheap: 2:1–13**
❸ **Wish I'd never been born!: 3:1–26**
❹ **What have I done wrong?: 6:1–21**
❺ **You're all talk: 15:1–35**
❻ **I will see God: 19:1–29**
❼ **Enter Elihu: 32:1–10; 33:1–33**
❽ **Enter God: 38:1–41**
❾ **Can you catch Leviathan?: 41:1–34**
❿ **Job's answer: 42:1–17**

Why does it matter?

Job lives in "the land of Uz", which is "somewhere in the East". In other words, he's not an Israelite. And that's appropriate, because this book asks a universal question: how can a good God allow innocent people to suffer? And the important thing about the book is that it rejects easy answers. Job and his friends want a nice, neat solution to why suffering occurs, but, in the end, God sweeps in, washing away all the arguments and the shallow theories with the reality of his power and presence. With its depth and power and beauty, Job is one of the greatest literary achievements in history.

Surprise me

One of the images that feature in the book is the creature Leviathan. This fire-breathing, ocean-dwelling monster is a symbolic representation of primeval chaos. And only God is strong enough to control him.

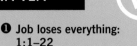

Sing a new song

What is it?

It's a poetry anthology. Or a songbook. Each "chapter" is a separate poem, composed at a different time, for a different purpose, and even by a different person. Brought together over at least 400 years, the book served as a prayer book for use in the Temple and synagogues. "Psalms" is a Greek word which comes from the psalterion, a kind of stringed instrument. It's a bit like calling the book "Guitaros".

Starring: The authors – David (73); Asaph (12); Sons of Korah (11); Solomon (2); Moses (1); Heman (1); Ethan (1); Anonymous (49)

@ **PSALMS**
Praise the Lord and pass the harp. It's the great Israelite songbook.

IN TEN

1. Trees by the riverbank: Psalm 1
2. The Lord is my rock: Psalm 18
3. Why have you forsaken me?: Psalm 22
4. The Lord is my shepherd: Psalm 23
5. The hunted deer: Psalm 42
6. Our refuge and strength: Psalm 46
7. Purify me: Psalm 51
8. Save me from my enemies: Psalm 107
9. I look up to the mountains: Psalm 121
10. Praise the Lord!: Psalm 150

What happens?

The 150 psalms cover subjects including war, peace, betrayal, loneliness, suffering, joy, and worship – all human life is here. And they fall into different categories. There are wisdom psalms, singing the praises of knowledge ❶. There are thanksgiving psalms, offering gratitude for God's works, for rescue ❷ or for answers to prayers. They may be giving thanks for a danger averted, a successful harvest, victory in battle, or God's goodness to the writer. Many psalms are laments or cries for help when the psalmist feels abandoned and hopeless ❸. These direct, passionate, emotional prayers often end with expressions of renewed faith in God and an acknowledgment that he is close ❹ and that the psalmist still has hope ❺. There are psalms that display confidence in God ❻ and psalms that plead for his mercy and compassion ❼.

There are also a number of painfully, unsettlingly honest psalms that curse either individuals or enemies of Israel. These dark psalms cry out for vengeance and yearn for the triumph and vindication of the Lord ❽.

Although most of the psalms praise God in some way, there are many that focus specifically on his greatness and power. A few psalms are pilgrimage songs or "songs of ascents", sung by people walking up the roads towards Jerusalem, or climbing the steps up to the Temple ❾. They may have been sung by pilgrims going to the city for one of the three annual festivals of Passover, Purim, and Sukkot. But the overwhelming theme of Psalms is praise. The Hebrew title is "Praises", and, though not all of the psalms fall into that category, the book as a whole undoubtedly celebrates and praises God – the God who is with us through all of life's joys and hardships ❿.

Why does it matter?

Psalms is one of the most emotional and "personal" books of the Bible. Reading it is often like peeking into someone's spiritual journal: one minute the air is full of praises; the next, everything is doom and despair. The raw honesty with which the psalmists face God is compelling and moving. This is why people still respond to these ancient poems. Because, thousands of years after they were written, we still experience the same feelings of joy and sadness, hopefulness and despair, worship, wonder, and praise.

Surprise me !

Thirty-nine of the psalms end with the word *selah*. No one knows for sure what this means. (It is also found in Habakkuk 3, which is a poem. And we don't know what it means there, either.)

A word to the wise

What is it?

It's a self-help book. Proverbs is a book of wisdom – but these aphorisms are not philosophical musings; they are supposed to be practical advice. The Hebrew concept of wisdom was closer to the idea of life skills. The book provides God's people with advice on how to live a godly life in an ungodly world.

@ PROVERBS

The fear of the Lord is the beginning of all wisdom (though reading Proverbs helps quite a lot as well).

What happens?

The book begins with an introduction about why wisdom is essential. These sayings will help the reader to do what is good, just, and fair. Only fools despise wisdom and instruction ❶. After this there is a section addressed to a young person, with each subsection beginning "my child". The image is of a father telling his child what he needs to know. It starts with a warning about choosing the right company, and then "wisdom" is personified as a woman calling for people to pay attention to her ❷. Wisdom is better than silver and gold; it's the very foundation of the earth ❸. Wisdom protects the young man from lures and temptations. It keeps him out of the embrace of the prostitute ❹. In a particularly striking passage,

Starring: The authors – Solomon, Agur the son of Jakeh, King Lemuel, and the person known only as "the Oracle"

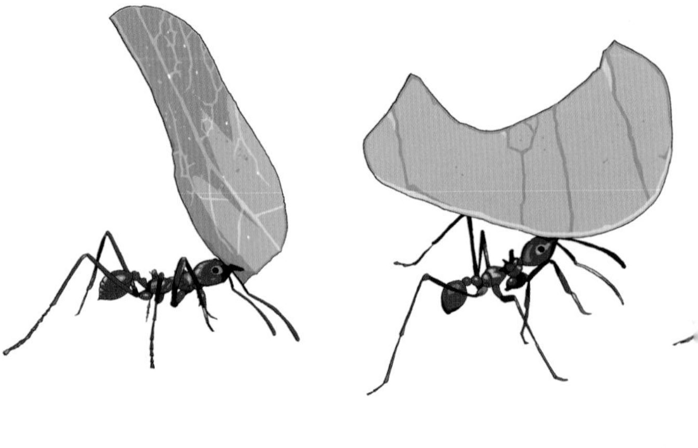

wisdom is depicted as being present at creation itself: it is represented as the oldest work of the creator ❺.

The second main section is a collection of proverbs attributed to Solomon. These are not really arranged thematically: they dart about from one subject to another, but the importance of respecting and obeying God is paramount ❻. Some themes recur: the value of hard work; the importance of controlling your speech ❼; the value of true friendship ❽; and respect for the poor and needy ❾. The final section contains proverbs from two otherwise unknown sages, Agur and Lemuel (or rather what was taught to Lemuel by his mother) ❿.

Why does it matter?

Proverbs is about the shaping of character. It is a book that is founded on the idea that people can change: wisdom can be learned. More, that wisdom should be cherished, collected, and celebrated. In our increasingly shallow culture, Proverbs is a corrective. It's a book that urges care and consideration, controlling your temper and your tongue, self-discipline and self-understanding.

IN TEN

❶ Instructions: 1:1–7
❷ Friends: 1:8–33
❸ Value of wisdom: 3:13–35
❹ Lured away: 7:1–27
❺ Words of wisdom: 8:12–36
❻ The Lord sees all: 15:1–33
❼ Language: 26:17 – 27:7
❽ True friendship: 27:17–27
❾ The poor: 28:1–28
❿ Sayings of Lemuel's mother: 31:1–31

Surprise me !

The Hebrew word for proverb can also mean "comparison" or even "taunt". In some ways that sums up this book; it's full of "provocations", nuggets of wisdom to make us think.

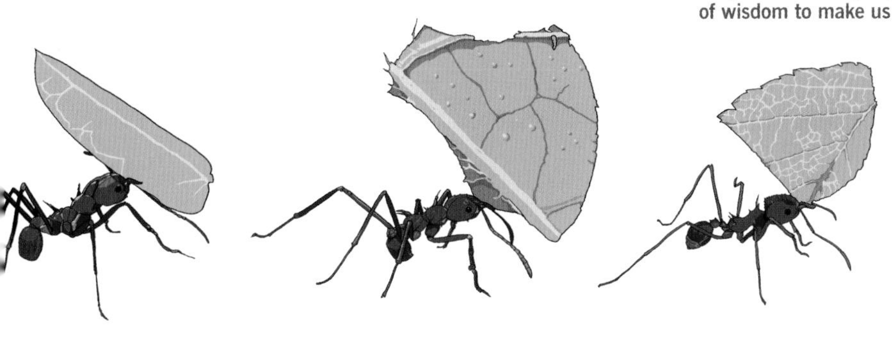

Everything is pointless

Starring: Koheleth (might be Solomon in disguise?)

What is it?

It's an art movie. In black and white. Very moody people in turtlenecks meditating on the meaning of life and ending with a Gallic shrug. Ecclesiastes is one of the most surprising books of the Bible: a cynical, weary summary of the apparent pointlessness of life. The "Teacher" looks at all of life – everything under the sun – and concludes that all is futile, pointless, and in vain.

@ ECCLESIASTES
What's the point, asks the Teacher. And he finds that there isn't one.

What happens?

Ecclesiastes is a book of two halves. The first part begins with an introduction from Koheleth – the Teacher. And the first line sums it up: everything is futile. There is nothing but an apparently meaningless cycle of life ❶. The Teacher tries enjoying himself, but that doesn't work. So he turns to the pursuit of wisdom, but in the end concludes only that, although it's better to be wise than foolish,

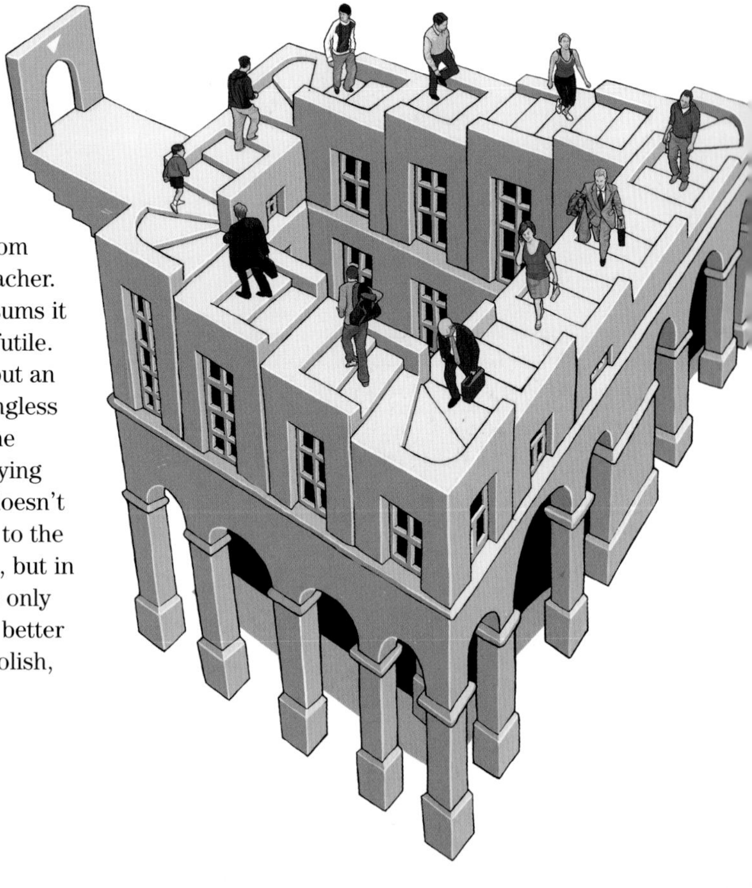

there is no happiness except in eating and drinking. In a beautiful passage of poetry, he concludes that everything has its time on earth and then returns to the dust from which it came ❷. He spends some time exploring the futility of human relationships, the desire for power, and even empty worship and prayer. There is so much injustice under the sun.

Part two begins with a reflection on wisdom. Rejecting hedonistic superficialities, the Teacher counsels wisdom, patience, and fortitude ❸. But, for all the emphasis on wisdom, in the end the fortunes of human life are beyond our understanding. Everyone has the same fate. The race is not won by the fastest and the wisest don't always get the rewards. So enjoy what you have; enjoy it while you are alive ❹. Finally the Teacher exhorts his listeners to remember their creator while they are young: God will call them to account one day. Old age will come calling and in the end, yes, you guessed it, everything is futile ❺.

IN FIVE

❶ **Nothing makes sense: 1:1–18**

❷ **A time for everything: 3:1–22**

❸ **Better an end than a beginning: 7:1–18**

❹ **The race is not always to the swiftest: 9:1–12**

❺ **Remember while you're young: 11:7 – 12:14**

Why does it matter?

It doesn't. Everything is meaningless. Oh, all right, then… Ecclesiastes contains some of the most moving, beautiful passages in scripture, but it is underlined throughout by a deep strain of cynicism, a penetrating rejection of superficial optimism and cheerful platitudes. But that's the point. That's exactly what gives Ecclesiastes its strength and power. It represents the thoughts of everyone who goes through those times of believing life to be pointless. Ecclesiastes is not a book that should be read in isolation from the rest of the Bible. It is a very partial picture. But it's very important that it is there, because it's how we all feel, sometimes.

Surprise me

The author – "Koheleth" or "Teacher" – is identified as "son of David, king of Jerusalem", which is usually taken to mean Solomon. However, it could mean a king from the line of Solomon, or even an ideal, archetypal king.

I'm in love with a Shulammite girl

Starring: The bridegroom, the bride, various gazelles, goats, lilies, apple trees, etc.

What is it?

It's a love song. Think soft focus, candlelight, champagne, wedding-night bliss, and a lot of heavy breathing. Because of its subject matter – and the absence of any mention of God – this book has worried both Jewish and Christian scholars. Many Jewish rabbis saw it as an allegory of the love between God and his people, while Christian teachers saw it as a picture of the love of Christ for his church, or even that between Christ and the believer's soul. The problem with these explanations is that there is no hint of them in the book itself, nor are similar metaphors found in the rest of the Bible. The fact is that Song of Songs is a celebration of one of God's most precious gifts: spontaneous and natural love. And that, surely, should be enough.

What happens?

There are five sections or poems and an epilogue, and each poem has a kind of dialogue going on between the man and the woman. In the first poem we are introduced to the woman: she is beautiful, but her skin is sun-darkened from working in the vineyards. She has been brought into the king's rooms to be his lover ❶. In the second poem it is springtime and the king is coming on a visit. She waits breathlessly in anticipation ❷. The third poem is a wedding song: the king comes in his splendour to take away his bride for her wedding day. She is like a private garden, where he will pick the finest fragrances, eat honeycomb, and drink wine ❸. The fourth poem begins with a troubled dream. Some time after the wedding, presumably, the

@ **SONGOFSONGS**
The girl from Shulam ♥ the king. The king ♥ the girl from Shulam. There is quite a lot about gazelles.

IN FIVE

5

- ❶ Love is better than wine: 1:1 – 2:7
- ❷ The visit: 2:8 – 3:5
- ❸ The wedding: 3:6 – 5:1
- ❹ The dream: 5:2 – 6:3
- ❺ Love is stronger than death: 7:12 – 8:7

bride has a dream in which she looks for the king but he is gone. Panicking, she searches through the streets for him. She is even mistaken for a prostitute and beaten by the city watchmen ❹. She takes comfort, though, in knowing that he belongs to her and she to him, wherever he is. The fifth poem is a statement of his love for her. She is valued above all his other brides and concubines. She tries to persuade him to return with her to her home in the country, to the fields and the vineyards. And, finally, in an epilogue, they declare that love is as strong as death, and passion more powerful than the grave ❺.

Why does it matter?

The Bible has a lot to say about the bad side of love and sex – from warnings against prostitutes to stories about lust and even rape. But Song of Songs celebrates the joy of physical love. Perhaps the most powerful voice in this poem is that of the woman, who speaks most profoundly of love, who affirms its spontaneity, power, and mystery.

Surprise me !

One of the features of the book that modern readers struggle with is the comparisons: the woman is compared to a horse in Pharaoh's court (1:9), she's got hair like a flock of goats (4:1), and a nose like a tower (7:4). In ancient poetry of this type these metaphors indicate quality: the comparison is usually a kind of absolute, a "best of". The horses in Pharaoh's court were the *best* horses in the world. So she's the best. (I recommend you don't try saying this at home, though.)

Judgment and restoration

What is it?

A threat and a promise. Isaiah is the first of the great books of prophecy in the Bible. The name Isaiah means "the Lord saves", and that sums up the theme of this work. It is a book about judgment and redemption. God will judge his people for their sins, but he will also rescue them from captivity. Set around the time of the Judean exile, political observations and historical accounts jostle with visions of the near and far future. And along with warnings to current kings there are many references to a future ruler, a messiah – the anointed one – who will rescue Israel and usher in a new age of peace and wholeness.

Starring: Isaiah, Ahaz, the Assyrians and the Babylonians, and featuring the child/heir of David/suffering servant as the messiah

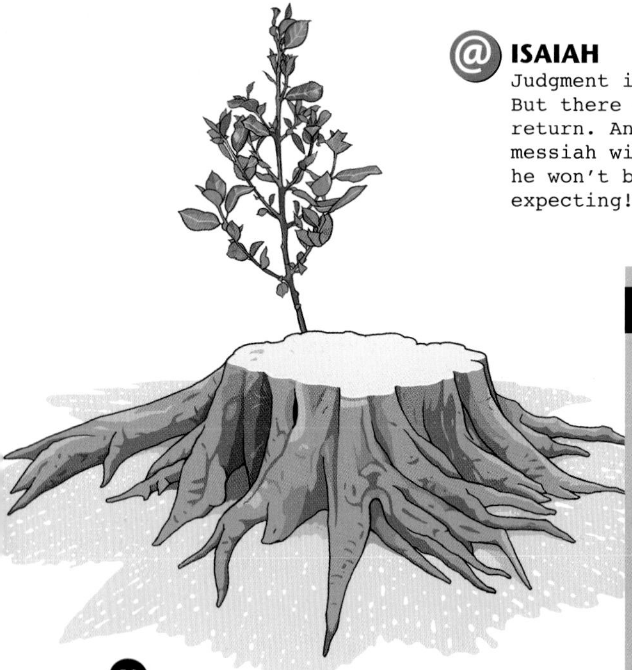

@ ISAIAH

Judgment is coming. But there will be a return. And one day the messiah will come (only he won't be what you're expecting!).

IN TEN

1. Justice, not religion: 1:1–20
2. The day of the Lord: 2:1–22
3. Immanuel: 7:10–17
4. A child is born: 9:1–7
5. The flowering wilderness: 35:1–10
6. Hezekiah's sin: 39:1–8
7. Build a highway: 40:1–31
8. Suffering servant: 53:1–12
9. True religion: 58:1–14
10. The new world: 65:17–25

What happens?

Isaiah starts with messages of condemnation ❶. First, he focuses on the Judeans and their ritualism and selfishness. The day of the Lord is coming, when God will judge all the world ❷. Then Isaiah starts talking about a messianic figure called Immanuel ("God with us") ❸; that Galilee of the Gentiles will be filled with glory and a child will be born ❹.

The focus then broadens as God proclaims judgment on nations such as Babylon, Assyria, and Egypt – all those countries surrounding or threatening Judah. This section closes with a vision of the restored kingdom: the wilderness will blossom, the blind will see, the deaf will hear, and the lame will leap for joy ❺. Then there is a brief interlude, looking back at the Assyrian invasion of 701 BC and telling the story of King Hezekiah. The king's prayers are answered and the nation escapes destruction by the Assyrians. But Hezekiah foolishly shows his treasures to the Babylonians, and one day they will come and attack ❻.

The third part of Isaiah opens with messages of comfort and hope. Babylon will overpower Judah, but there will be restoration. A highway will be built in the wilderness: God is coming back! ❼ Then Isaiah introduces a figure who will usher in a kingdom of peace. He will also be a suffering servant ❽. God calls on his people to show true repentance and live lives of justice ❾. One day, he says, the glory of Jerusalem will be restored. From all around the world people will find blessing in the city. The messiah will reign and God will make all things new ❿.

Why does it matter?

Isaiah contains some of the most important, inspiring, moving, and powerful passages in the Bible. From Isaiah we get some of the most striking pictures of the messiah: the suffering servant, the prince of peace, the one who will bring healing and restoration. It is a book that constantly emphasizes both God's justice and his mercy, and which looks forward to a time when the land will be healed, when there will be no more suffering, sadness, or pain.

Surprise me !

Isaiah has two sons: Shear-Jashub (7:3) and the snappily named Maher-Shalal-Hash-Baz (8:3). These names are signs: they mean "a remnant will return" and "quick to the plunder, swift to the spoil".

We're all doomed!

What is it?

It's a disaster movie. And the disaster is Babylon, coming for Judah like Godzilla on the rampage. Well, God, rather than Godzilla... Jeremiah's message is that, unless they change their ways, God will punish the kingdom of Judah and its capital, Jerusalem. That's an unpopular message, and Jeremiah suffers for it; he is thrown into jail, publicly humiliated, and even dumped in a water-storage cistern (fortunately at the time it held only mud).

Starring: Jeremiah, Baruch (his secretary); Kings Josiah, Zedekiah, Shallum, Jehoiakim, and Jehoiachin; various false prophets. And featuring Nebuchadnezzar as "Babylonian ruler with enormous army"

IN TEN

10

1. God chooses Jeremiah: 1:1–19
2. First message: 2:1–37
3. In the Temple: 7:1 – 8:3
4. Mouldy underwear: 13:1–27
5. Do not marry: 16:1–18
6. Seventy years: 25:1–14
7. The false prophet: 27:1–8; 28:1–17
8. The new agreement: 31:1–40
9. Down the sewer: 38:1–28
10. The end: 39:1–14

@ JEREMIAH

Doom is coming. And it's your own fault. No good blocking me, just because you don't like what I say. Seventy years of exile are on their way.

What happens?

God calls Jeremiah during the reign of a good king, Josiah ❶. But even Josiah's reforms can't stem the tide of idolatry and disbelief, and his successors pursue political policies and religious practices that bring disaster. Jeremiah compares Judah to a young bride who has turned into an adulteress, or a thief who feels shame only when he is caught ❷. Jeremiah stands in the Temple and accuses the Jews of hypocrisy. They are doomed ❸. He is told to perform a number of symbolic actions, such as wearing a linen loincloth and then hiding it in a hole by the Euphrates until it is mildewed and useless (it's a symbol of what will happen to Judah) ❹. He is forbidden to marry or have children because they will only die from war or famine ❺. He buys a pot and smashes it, and wears a yoke as a symbol of captivity. All these and his predictions of seventy years of exile ❻ bring opposition from the people and from false prophets ❼. But he's right. Babylon attacks and deports the first lot of exiles. Jeremiah speaks of restoration and rebuilding. God will make a new agreement with his people, one written in their hearts ❽. As the final disaster looms and Jerusalem is besieged, Jeremiah is thrown down a cistern ❾. He is released, and Jerusalem is captured ❿. Jeremiah is taken to Egypt by Jews escaping the carnage, but he prophesies that the Babylonians will capture Egypt as well. The book ends with a series of oracles to the nations and a final historical account of the fall of Jerusalem.

Why does it matter?

As well as giving us a unique insight into the final, doomed days of Judah, Jeremiah is a very honest book. The prophet is an anxious figure and he often struggles with his calling (not surprising when you see what happened to him). There are many calls for vengeance, and many tears. At one of the lowest points he is instructed to buy a field: it is a metaphor, a sign that one day the people will return to their land. He keeps the memory of his first calling close to his heart and he keeps going. While all around him collapses, Jeremiah's foundations remain firm.

Surprise me

Jeremiah prophesied for nearly fifty years. From 627–605 BC he worked while Judah was threatened by Assyria and Egypt; from 605–586 BC he proclaimed God's judgment against Babylon, and from 586–580 BC he prophesied while the city was captured.

We've lost everything!

What is it?

If you've ever seen people devastated by grief or loss, this book is the equivalent. It's the funeral song of a city. In 588 BC the army of the Babylonian empire overran Judah and destroyed the city of Jerusalem. The Judean people were taken away into exile in Babylon and their treasured city, the city of David, was left in ruins. Lamentations, traditionally attributed to the prophet Jeremiah, consists of five poems reflecting the chaos and despair.

@ **LAMENTATIONS**
The funeral of Jerusalem. Overwhelming grief. God has left the building. Will he ever come back?

☆

Starring: Jerusalem, as the bereaved widow

What happens?

It begins with a widow sobbing, grief-stricken. She is the personification of Jerusalem, the holy city, the former queen of nations. She has been betrayed by her friends, taken into exile, reduced to a slave because of her immorality and sin ❶. The second poem reveals who has done this: it is the Lord. God has become like an

enemy to the land and its inhabitants. He has even destroyed the Temple. It is God's anger that has done this. He has punished the city and its lying prophets, who, instead of pointing out sins, gave promises of false hope. He has carried out what he was threatening to do ❷. Then, in the middle of the book, the third poem brings a brief shaft of light. Despite his suffering, the poet (Jeremiah?) has confidence in God. Amid his loss and darkness he still dares to hope. He reminds himself that God's love never ceases, his mercy never comes to an end ❸. But after this it is back into the darkness with a bleak, horrific description of the conditions of the siege ❹. The poet ends with a cry for restoration and the poem finishes with the terrifying question: "Has God utterly rejected us? What if he's still angry?" ❺

Surprise me !

Four of the poems in Lamentations are acrostics, with each verse, or section, beginning with successive letters of the Hebrew alphabet. It's as if you wrote a poem in which the first sentence begins with "A", the second with "B", the third with "C", and so on. It's as if their suffering has gone from A–Z, across the complete range of experience.

Why does it matter?

Lamentations, more than any book in the Bible, is for anyone whose life is in ruins. This is a poem about complete and utter loss. The Hebrew name for the book is simply "Alas", which sums it up perfectly. The Babylonians are never mentioned: this is God's doing. Yet despite all this the prophet dares to hope that the Lord will build up his city and his people again.

IN FIVE

❶ The weeping widow: 1:1–22
❷ The angry God: 2:1–22
❸ Hope in the ruins: 3:1–66
❹ Jerusalem's punishment: 4:1–22
❺ Mercy!: 5:1–22

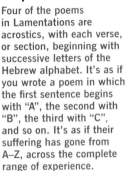

What on earth are you trying to say?

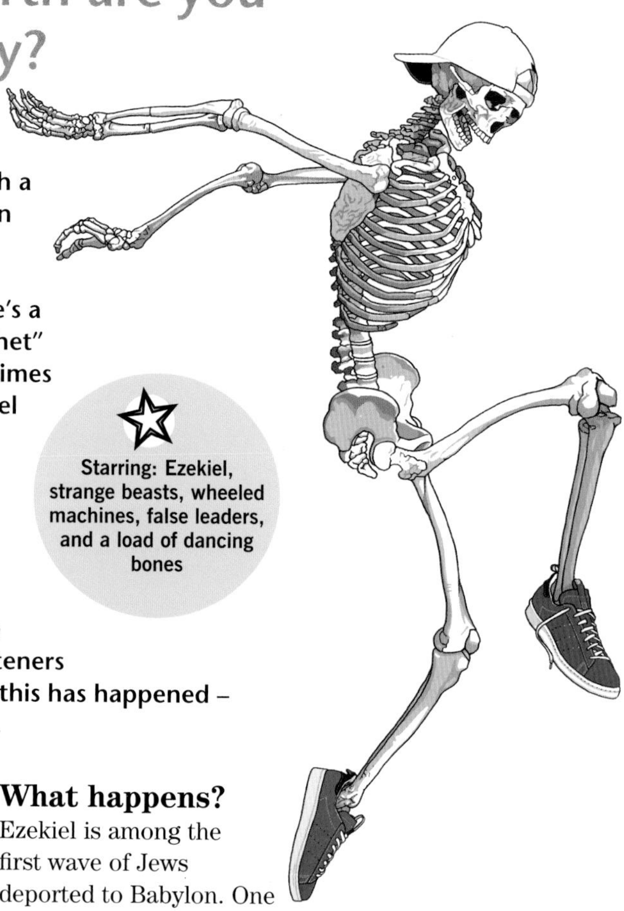

What is it?

He's a stunt-prophet with a bit of psychedelia thrown in. Ezekiel is one of the most thrillingly bizarre books of the Bible. There's a thin line between "prophet" and "nutter", and sometimes it seems as though Ezekiel has crossed that line. But Ezekiel was among the first group of people from Judah to be deported to Babylon, and his actions, along with his vivid visions, are designed to shock his listeners into understanding why this has happened – and what is still to come.

Starring: Ezekiel, strange beasts, wheeled machines, false leaders, and a load of dancing bones

@ EZEKIEL

He acts like a madman, but Ezekiel has a message for all Israel. Jerusalem has acted like a whore, but one day things will be different.

What happens?

Ezekiel is among the first wave of Jews deported to Babylon. One day he sees a powerful vision of heaven, with strange multi-faced, winged creatures and revolving, sparkling wheels. A human-like figure commands Ezekiel to speak to the nation of Israel ❶. This figure gives Ezekiel a scroll, which the prophet eats, and all the messages sink deep into his heart ❷.

Ezekiel begins to act out the destruction of Jerusalem to those around him. His deeds include lying down on one side and then on the other for many days ("one day for each year of Judah's sin"), cutting off his hair ❸, and acting out the flight from Jerusalem by breaking a hole in the wall of his house and escaping through it ❹. In brutal, shocking language he likens Jerusalem to a prostitute ❺. He depicts Jerusalem as a rusted pot which must be scorched to clean it of corruption. Shockingly, he is forbidden even to mourn for his wife – a sign that the people are to mourn inwardly for all they have done ❻. Ezekiel is a watchman for his people ❼. He raises the alarm about the leaders of the Jews, likening them to good and bad shepherds ❽.

In a vision of restoration, he sees a valley of dry, sun-bleached bones brought back to life by the Spirit of God ❾. The final section of Ezekiel is an extended vision of a restored Israel and a rebuilt Temple, from the centre of which a river issues to bring new life to all the people ❿.

IN TEN

10

- ❶ Ezekiel is chosen: 1:1 – 2:10
- ❷ Eat the scroll: 3:1–27
- ❸ Acts of destruction: 4:1–17
- ❹ Through the wall: 12:1–16
- ❺ Jerusalem sleeps around: 16:1–43
- ❻ The rusty pot: 24:1–27
- ❼ Ezekiel the watchman: 33:21–33
- ❽ Good and bad shepherds: 34:1–31
- ❾ The valley of bones: 37:1–28
- ❿ The stream from the Temple: 47:1–12

Why does it matter?

Ezekiel had to shock people out of their complacency and apathy. Sometimes God's messages have to be brought to people in a way that they cannot ignore. Ezekiel's messages are couched in violent, almost obscene language, or played out in dramatic, bizarre actions. He is passionate, because God is passionate. He outrages people because God wants to shock them out of their apathy, to get them to open their eyes.

Surprise me

Because of its extreme nature, Ezekiel was one of the last books to be admitted into the Jewish scriptures. Some rabbis restricted access to parts of the book to those over thirty!

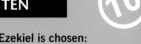

Keep the faith

What is it?

Part folk tale, part apocalyptic vision. The first half tells how the faith of Daniel and his friends helps them to prosper during captivity in Babylon. The second half is a full-on Jewish apocalyptic prophecy about future empires, angelic powers, and times of trial.

☆

Starring: Episode 1: Daniel, Shadrach, Meshach, Abednego, Nebuchadnezzar, Belshazzar, and Darius the Mede. Episode 2: Daniel, the Ancient of Days, various beasts, goats, rams, and the angels Gabriel and Michael

What happens?

Daniel is among a group of Jews taken into exile in Babylon, where he refuses to compromise his faith. When the Babylonian emperor Nebuchadnezzar has a dream, only Daniel can interpret it ❶. Nebuchadnezzar orders people to worship his statue, but three of Daniel's friends – Shadrach, Meshach, and Abednego – refuse. Thrown into a furnace, they survive unharmed, aided by a mysterious fourth figure ❷. Nebuchadnezzar has another dream (again interpreted by Daniel) and descends into madness, walking on all fours and eating grass. His sanity returns only when he acknowledges God. Nebuchadnezzar's successor, Belshazzar, holds a feast during which a mysterious hand writes on the wall. Daniel interprets the message: Belshazzar has been weighed and found wanting. That night Darius the Mede conquers Babylon ❸. Darius orders everyone in his kingdom to pray to him. Daniel refuses and is thrown to the lions, but is unharmed ❹.

In the second part of the book, Daniel has a series of visions concerning future empires. He sees four strange beasts representing four world powers, and an "Ancient of Days" who judges them. An angel (Gabriel) describes a succession of kings ruling over Israel, culminating in one who will abolish the sacrifices and desecrate the Temple ❺. This leader will be defeated and the dead will come back to life and be judged.

DANIEL

Am in Lions' Den. Others in fiery furnace. Probably going to turn out all right, though. Wonder what the future holds?

IN FIVE

5

1. Nebuchadnezzar's dream: 2:1–49
2. The fiery furnace: 3:1–30
3. The writing on the wall: 5:1–31
4. The lions' den: 6:1–28
5. Abomination: 11:25–35

Why does it matter?

Daniel is about faithful Jews resisting pressure to compromise or abandon their faith. It also contains important prophecies to do with the Messiah. Its message is that those who remain faithful will be vindicated.

Surprise me !

Daniel is written in two languages: Hebrew and Aramaic. It's the only extended piece of writing in Aramaic in the Bible. The evil king described in Daniel's visions is Antiochus IV Epiphanes (175–164 BC), who attempted to expunge the Jewish faith and even sacrificed a pig (an unclean animal) in the Temple.

The unfaithful wife

IN FIVE

5

❶ Wife and children: 1:1 – 2:1
❷ Gomer is redeemed: 3:1–5
❸ Wilful refusal: 8:1–14
❹ Attack and destroy: 13:1–11
❺ Future forgiveness: 14:1–9

What is it?

A tragic romance. Hosea is told to marry an unfaithful prostitute called Gomer in order to symbolise God's enduring love for Israel.

What happens?

Hosea is told to marry Gomer – whom he loves, but who spends her time sleeping around. She bears him three children. God tells Hosea to name them Jezreel ("God-scattered"), Lo-Ruhamah ("not loved"), and Lo-Ammi ("not my people") ❶. Gomer deserts Hosea and is taken into slavery. God says that, like Gomer, Israel will be shamed, but that he will speak tenderly to her and win her back. Signifying this, Hosea buys Gomer back from the slave market ❷. The rest of the book accuses the Israelites of worshipping idols and wilfully turning away from God ❸. They will be scattered, the land will be barren, and the cities will be destroyed ❹. Despite this, God continues to love Israel. He cannot let them go and one day he will restore their land ❺.

Starring: Hosea, Gomer, Jezreel, Lo-Ruhamah, and Lo-Ammi

@ HOSEA

`I'm off to buy my wife back from the slave market. Despite all she's done, I still love her. Just like God with Israel.`

Why does it matter?

This is one of the most remarkable images of God's love in the Bible. Hosea really lives out his message: despite the depravity of Israel and its unfaithfulness, God will not give up on it. There will be punishment, but, just as Hosea redeems Gomer, so God will redeem Israel.

Surprise me

The big sin of Israel? Idolatry. Of some 150 statements Hosea makes concerning the sins of Israel, over half of them are to do with idolatry.

Simply... **JOEL**

Locusts! Locusts!! LOCUSTS!!!

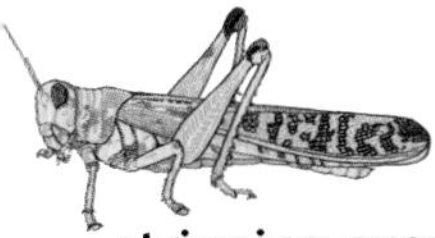

What is it?

It's an explanation. A plague of locusts has descended on Judah, stripping everything bare. Joel explains that this is a judgment on sin, and, what is more, God's eventual judgment will make the locusts seem like nothing.

What happens?

A vast army of locusts has descended on Judah, eating everything in its path ❶. This causes a drought and a famine ❷. Joel sees it as a prophecy of imminent invasion by a much more dangerous army ❸. And the only insect repellent that will work against this army is for the people to return to their God. Then God will pour out his Spirit again on his people ❹. Joel goes on to talk about a further judgment, the day of the Lord, when God will judge the nations and restore Judah to a life-giving refuge and fortress ❺.

Starring: Joel, the locusts, and an unnamed army

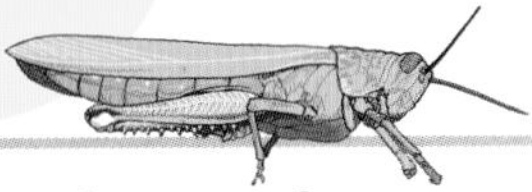

Why does it matter?

The dominant theme in Joel is the arrival of the "day of the Lord". On that day, God will put things right. He will restore his people, bring abundance and safety to them and dwell with them. This was a significant prophecy for the New Testament followers of Jesus, who believed that it had come to fruition in Jesus. In his talk to the crowd at Pentecost, Peter quotes from Joel 2:28–32.

IN FIVE

❶ The day of the locust: 1:1–12

❷ The day of drought: 1:13–20

❸ Invasion warning: 2:1–11

❹ Turn around: 2:12–32

❺ Judgment and restoration: 3:1–21

@ JOEL

An army of locusts will be followed by a real army, and, eventually, by the day of the Lord.

Surprise me

We don't know when Joel was written. It could be anywhere from the ninth century to the fourth century BC.

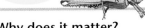

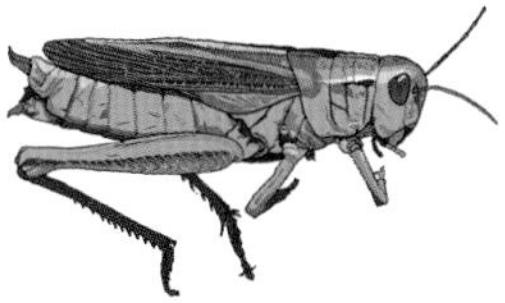

I hate your religion!

What is it?

It's street preaching. Amos delivers a stinging attack on the hypocritical, superficial leaders and residents of the northern kingdom of Israel. They pretend to be holy, but their society is crawling with idolatry, corruption, and injustice.

What happens?

Amos is called to prophesy against the leaders and people of Israel. He starts by issuing judgment on Israel's neighbours: Damascus, Philistia, Phoenicia, Edom, Ammon, and Judah ❶. But then he talks of God's judgment on Israel for their corruption and treatment of the poor ❷. Samaria (the capital of Israel) will be crushed. The rich women of the city – fat cows of Bashan, he calls them – will be herded away ❸. Amos says that God hates their superficial religion and their selfish lifestyle ❹. He predicts that Israel will be destroyed, but in the future the house of David will be restored ❺.

IN FIVE 5

❶ Judgment on nations: 1:1 – 2:5

❷ Judgment on Israel: 2:6–16

❸ You fat cows!: 4:1–13

❹ I hate your religion: 5:21–27

❺ The house of David: 9:1–15

Starring: Amos, Amaziah, and the fat cows of Samaria

REPENT!
DOMESDAY
IS NEAR!

@ AMOS

```
You selfish cows! You hypocritical priests! You smug rich people! God hates your hypocritical religion. Act justly or God will punish you!
```

Why does it matter?

Amos preached in the reign of King Jeroboam, a golden age for the northern kingdom of Israel. But Amos claims their wealth has nothing to do with divine favour: it's the result of abusing the poor and cheating the oppressed. God hates empty religion and meaningless rituals: what he wants is justice and mercy.

How could you?

What is it?

It's a threatening note. This brief prophecy deals with the destruction of Edom, a nation south of the Dead Sea. It should have supported Israel during an invasion (probably the destruction of Jerusalem in 586 BC), but didn't. For that reason it will be punished.

What happens?

It begins with a warning from God: Edom will be made the least among nations because of its arrogance and the way it has behaved. Not a single person will survive ❶. The Edomites' crime? They stood by while Jerusalem was ransacked; they watched as the people of Judah fled ❷. But the day of the Lord will come. The other nations will be destroyed, but the house of Jacob and Joseph will survive ❸.

IN THREE

❶ You will be destroyed: 1:1–9

❷ You did nothing: 1:10–14

❸ I will survive: 1:15–21

Surprise me

With only two hundred and ninety-one words in the original Hebrew, Obadiah is the shortest book in the Bible. To put that in context, if you add together all the words on this page, you will find there are exactly the same number as there are in Obadiah. So there you go.

@ OBADIAH

```
You saw what they were
doing and did nothing!
You just stood by. For
that, God will utterly
destroy you & any other
nation that does the same!
```

Starring: Obadiah and Edom. Er... That's it, really

Why does it matter?

Jews believe that Edomites are descended from Esau, Jacob's brother, so this is not just nation vs nation: this is family. But "Edom" also stands for other nations as well; the second part of the prophecy implies that all the "other" nations will be judged on the day of the Lord.

A fishy tale

Starring: Jonah, the sailors, the people of Nineveh and, of course, the fish

What is it?

An animated cartoon starring a pompous prophet, the most evil nation in the world, and a large "fish". This is a story *about* a prophet, rather than a book of prophecy. Jonah is a successful prophet (in 2 Kings 14:25 he predicts success to King Jeroboam II). But then he's told to go and tell the most wicked city on earth to repent. (Imagine being told to go to Berlin in 1936 and tell the Nazis to repent and you get the idea.) Is Jonah fact or fiction? Whatever the case, it's a wonderful story, with moments of both deep comedy and profound truth.

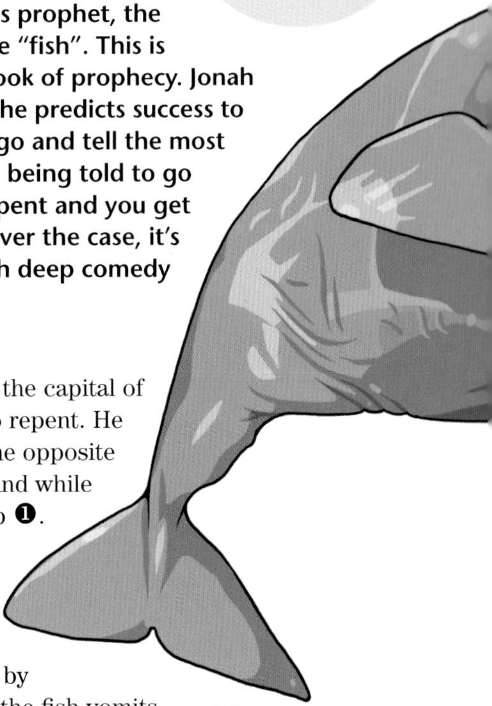

What happens?

Jonah is given a message: go to Nineveh – the capital of the Assyrian empire – and tell its people to repent. He does the only obvious thing: he heads in the opposite direction and boards a ship for Tarshish. And while Jonah sleeps below decks a storm blows up ❶. The sailors draw lots to find out who is "responsible" for the storm, but Jonah knows it is him and tells them to throw him overboard. Reluctantly, they do ❷. He is not drowned, though, but swallowed by a fish. In the belly of the fish he prays and the fish vomits him up onto dry land ❸. God repeats his instruction to Jonah and this time the prophet obeys. He goes to Nineveh and tells them to repent. Amazingly, they do so ❹. This makes Jonah angry: he doesn't *want* the Assyrians to be forgiven. He sits outside the city and the Lord gives him a plant for shade. Then the Lord sends a worm to destroy the plant and the heat becomes such that Jonah wants to die. "If you cared so much about the plant," says God, "shouldn't I care more about the people of Nineveh?" ❺

@

JONAH

Jonah given task. Jonah runs away. Jonah swallowed by fish. Jonah does task. People repent. Jonah unhappy. How can God love foreigners?

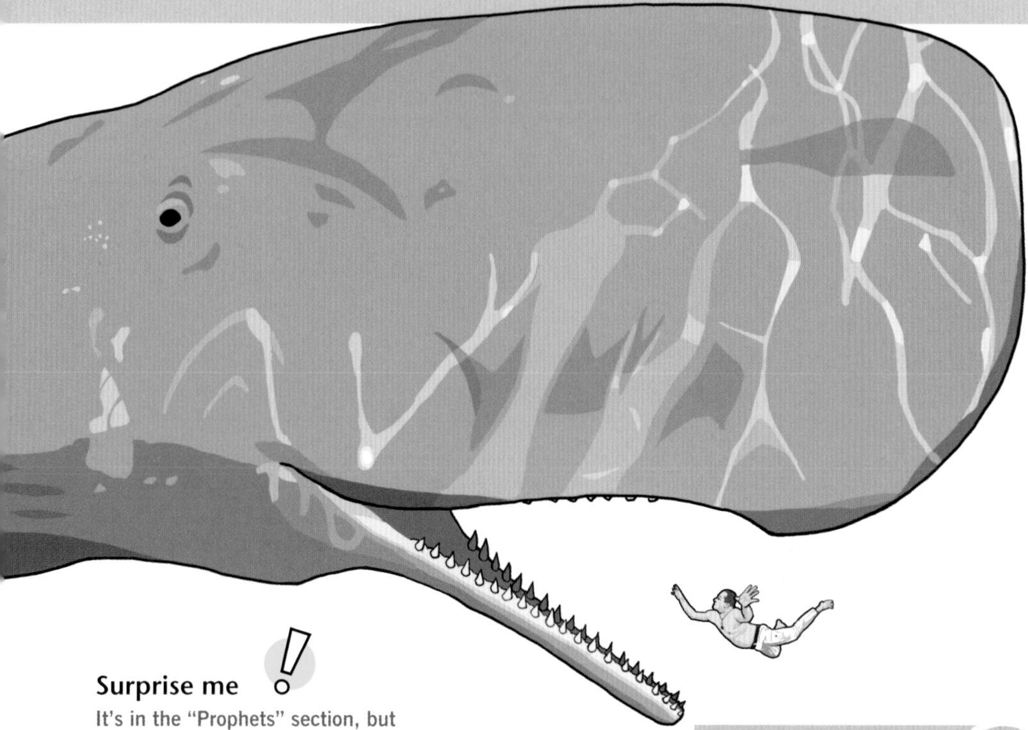

Surprise me

It's in the "Prophets" section, but Jonah contains only one line of actual prophecy: "Forty more days and Nineveh will be overturned."

Why does it matter?

We tend to retell it as a children's story, but this is one of the most profound statements about God's love in the entire Scripture. The surprise is not that Jonah ran away; it's that God wants to forgive the Assyrians. How could God care about people who were trying to destroy the Israelites? In that sense, the debate about whether Jonah is real or not misses the point. The point is that God loves everyone. The hated, feared Assyrians are God's children as well. So it's not just Jonah's courage that is being tested; it's his entire view of God.

IN FIVE

❶ **Jonah runs away: 1:1–8**
❷ **Man overboard: 1:9–16**
❸ **In the belly of the fish: 2:1–10**
❹ **The Assyrians repent: 3:1–10**
❺ **All people matter: 4:1–11**

Out of Bethlehem

@ **MICAH**

You corrupt, greedy, unjust rulers! You'll be punished! One day a true, just, peaceful ruler will arrive. (BTW: he's coming from Bethlehem.)

What is it?

It's a kind of lawsuit. Micah brings "charges" against Israel and Judah. He rails against injustice and calls on the people to change their ways. And he says that a future king will bring peace.

What happens?

Micah says that the day of the Lord is coming and judgment is on its way ❶. He outlines their sins: idol worship, greed, and theft of property. They hate good and love evil. But one day there will be justice and peace ❷. From Bethlehem there will come a true ruler who will bring peace and security ❸. Never mind all their sacrifices; God requires justice, humility, and kindness. So for their sins there will be destruction, but one day there will also be restoration and hope.

Starring: Micah and a future ruler

IN THREE 3

- ❶ Judgment: 1:1–16
- ❷ Swords into ploughshares: 4:1–5
- ❸ Out of Bethlehem: 5:2–5

Surprise me !

Micah grew up in a village – Moresheth in southern Judah, about 22 miles (35 km) south-west of Jerusalem. This probably gave him more sympathy for ordinary folk who had lost their land.

Why does it matter?

Micah is a source of some of the most important prophecies about the messiah. Like his contemporary, Amos, he condemns the injustice and corruption of the ruling elite. But he also paints a promise of future hope. Out of Bethlehem there will come a true ruler, a man of peace, who will feed his flock in the strength of the Lord.

A warning to Nineveh

Starring: Nahum, citizens of Nineveh, invading soldiers, etc.

What is it?

It's a disaster alert. A severe weather warning. The book describes the destruction of Nineveh, capital of the Assyrian empire. It will be washed away.

What happens?

Nahum of Elkosh delivers a warning to Nineveh: the avenging God is on his way, powerful enough to destroy mountains and dry up seas ❶. The chaos in the city will be unequalled. Chariots race through the streets, the river gates are open; Nineveh is like a pool being drained, everything is washing away ❷. The city of bloodshed will be utterly devastated. Just as the Egyptian city of Thebes has been destroyed, so Nineveh will be mortally wounded, and those who have suffered at her hands will simply applaud ❸.

@ NAHUM

```
Red alert! Bye bye,
Assyria. The storm
is coming and God
is going to wash
you away.
```

IN THREE

❶ **Storms and whirlwinds: 1:1–6**
❷ **All washed up: 2:1–13**
❸ **City of bloodshed: 3:1–19**

Why does it matter?

God is depicted in Nahum as slow but sure. He is "slow to anger" but his power is enormous. Evil will not triumph. The city that had more merchants than stars in the sky (3:16) – all this will be blown away.

Surprise me !

The Assyrian emperor Sennacherib built a magnificent palace in Nineveh, surrounded by redirected rivers and a huge wall. Nahum depicts the river gates bursting and the Euphrates river flooding the city (2:6).

Simply... **HABAKKUK**

Why?

What is it?

It's an argument. Or a dialogue at least. Judah was in turmoil. So Habakkuk asks God: why are you allowing this to happen? The question is worked out in two "dialogues" between the prophet and God, before Habakkuk concludes with a prayer-like psalm.

IN THREE

1. **It's unbelievable: 1:1–11**
2. **As the waters cover the sea: 1:12 – 2:20**
3. **Waiting for the day: 3:1–19**

What happens?

Habakkuk cries out to God, "Why all this destruction and violence? Where is the justice?" "You would not believe it if you were told," replies God. The Babylonians are God's agents ❶. "But how can God allow such evil?" asks Habakkuk. "How can such a pure being allow such impurity?" "Write this down," says God. "Injustice will be punished. Arrogance will be humbled; towns built on bloodshed will be demolished; the earth will know the glory of the Lord" ❷. In response, Habakkuk acknowledges God's glory. God will be victorious and Habakkuk has confidence in him ❸.

@ HABAKKUK

`Habakkuk asks "Why"? God explains that the wicked must be punished. He recognizes God's power and waits for the day of the Lord.`

Why does it matter?

Habakkuk deals with similar issues to Job, but where Job asks, "How could you let this happen to *me*?" Habakkuk asks, "How could you let this happen to *us*?" Habakkuk's question results, in the end, in an acknowledgment of God's power and a moving and passionate declaration of faith.

The day of the Lord is coming!

What is it?

A wake-up call. Zephaniah prophesied in the reign of King Josiah of Judah, under whom there was a national revival. So it's possible that Zephaniah was that rarity: a prophet who was listened to. He tells the people of Judah that the day of the Lord is coming. They believe this would be the moment when the Lord would wipe out all their enemies. But Zephaniah tells them that Judah will also get what it deserves.

IN THREE 3

- ❶ **Judgment in Jerusalem: 1:1 – 2:3**
- ❷ **Deserted, literally: 2:4–15**
- ❸ **The return of the king: 3:1–20**

What happens?

Starring: Zephaniah, Josiah, and the people of Jerusalem

The day of the Lord is at hand! And it won't be good for Judah. God will sweep away idolatrous priests and violent, fraudulent citizens. Jerusalem will be plundered, because people have sinned ❶. Other nations, too, will be deserted and laid waste: Philistia, Moab, Ammon, Ethiopia, even Assyria – they will be like Sodom and Gomorrah, like dried-up deserts ❷. Jerusalem is a wicked city: it will be punished. But one day it will be restored. It will sing again. The lame and the outcast will be saved. The king will return ❸.

@

ZEPHANIAH

It's the day of the Lord! But that's not necessarily a good thing for Judah.

Surprise me !

Zephaniah, son of Cushi, was a distant member of the royal family; his great-great-grandfather was King Hezekiah.

Why does it matter?

The Judeans thought that God was inevitably on their side and that the day of the Lord would be just about punishing their enemies. But Zephaniah shows us that everyone has to clean up their act. No one escapes judgment.

Keep going

@ HAGGAI
What's with the Temple? Why has the work stopped? Haggai urges the people to rebuild the Temple. It will be even better than before.

What is it?

It's a series of motivational speeches given in 520 BC to formerly exiled Jews who are finding life hard back in Jerusalem. Haggai urges them to review their priorities, to lay aside economic concerns and to get the Temple going again.

IN THREE

❶ Get going!: 1:1–15
❷ Better than before: 2:1–9
❸ My signet ring: 2:20–23

What happens?

In Jerusalem, the people are cold, hungry, and weary. Haggai says this is because they have given up rebuilding the Temple. The people start work again ❶. Six weeks later Haggai tells them that the Temple doesn't look much, but it will be more splendid than its predecessor ❷. Two months later, Haggai gives two visionary messages. First, the people's concentration on their own interests has tainted the rebuilding process. Second, in the far future, God will shake the heavens and the earth. The work will be completed one day ❸.

Starring: Haggai, Zerubbabel, and Joshua the high priest

Surprise me

We can date the book of Haggai with amazing precision. Haggai had four visions, all in the second year of King Darius (i.e. 520 BC). They were on the first day of the sixth month, the twenty-first day of the seventh month, and the twenty-fourth day of the ninth month (when he had two visions). That's 29 August, 17 October, and 18 December to be precise!

Why does it matter?

Haggai's messages are about priorities. In the struggle for existence, the people have forgotten that God should be central. Put God at the core, says Haggai, attend to the rebuilding of the Temple, and everything else will fall into place.

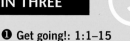

The messiah is on his way

What is it?

It's part exhortation, part vision: Ezekiel-lite. Zechariah urges the people to rebuild the Temple and to obey God's commands. But he also weaves together narratives, visions, and oracles to point to the messiah, a figure who will be the true anointed ruler of Israel.

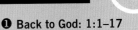

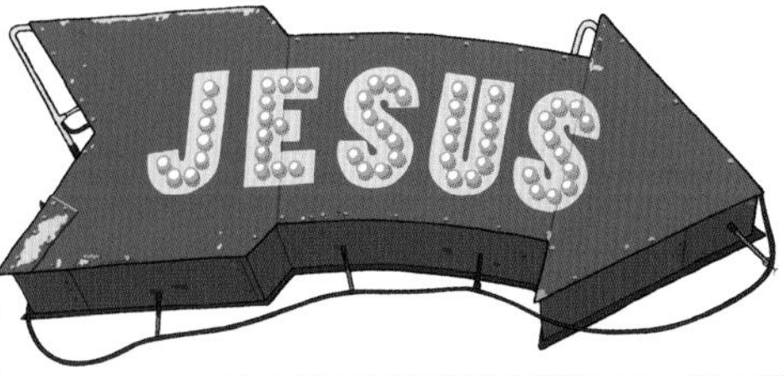

What happens?

Zechariah calls people back to God ❶. He has eight strange visions including a plumb line measuring the city ❷, a seven-branched lamp stand lit by two olive trees, and a flying scroll. Some visions are about the power of the Lord; some are to do with the rebuilding of the Temple and the status of King Zerubbabel and Joshua the high priest as anointed leaders.

The prophet condemns hypocritical fasting and religious observance. There is a series of oracles against Israel's enemies and messages of victory and restoration. A messiah will come, a ruler like no other. He will ride on a donkey ❸. He will come from the house of David, but he will also be wounded ❹. Finally, Zechariah sees a battle, in which the forces of the Lord defeat his enemies. Jerusalem becomes the centre of the world and all people go there for the festivals. Gentile and Jew will worship the Lord ❺.

IN FIVE (5)

❶ Back to God: 1:1–17
❷ Plumb line: 2:1–13
❸ On a donkey: 9:9–17
❹ Wounded shepherd: 12:10 – 13:1
❺ Everything is holy: 14:1–21

@

ZECHARIAH
Jerusalem will be rebuilt. But in the future there will come another leader – the messiah. And then God will be worshipped by everyone.

Why does it matter?

No prophet has more to say about the messiah, or points more clearly to Jesus. Zechariah saw a wounded king, a shepherd for whom all creation was waiting. He saw what was coming and his excitement and awe shine through in virtually every line.

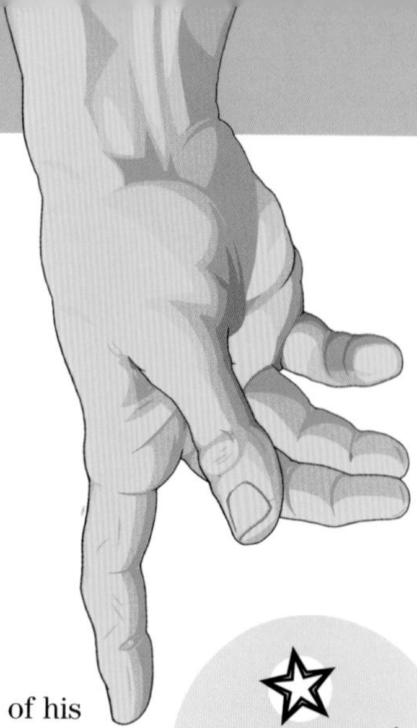

Someone is coming...

What is it?

It's a series of arguments. In rapid-fire dialogue, God accuses the people and the people accuse God. The Temple, far from being a spiritual powerhouse, is a place where people simply go through the ritual. The glory prophesied by Zechariah and Haggai some ninety years before has not come about.

IN THREE

❶ God loves Israel: 1:1–5
❷ Lack of respect: 1:6 – 2:9
❸ The day of the Lord: 4:1–5

What happens?

God reassures the people of his love for them ❶. But they don't respect him: they offer him improper sacrifices and inadequate offerings ❷. Like an unfaithful wife, they have not kept their promises. So God will send a messenger to them, to purify them, refine them. The messenger will precede the day of the Lord. God will send Elijah before that day to tell people to repent ❸.

Starring: Malachi

@ MALACHI

"I love you," says God. "But you don't respect me. I'm going to send a messenger, Elijah. And then things will really get interesting."

Why does it matter?

Malachi reminds people that religious ritual has value only if it is a true expression of sincere belief. The Law only matters if people obey it. He points to a messenger still to come. Someone whom the people will believe to be Elijah and who will call for repentance. The followers of Jesus interpreted this as John the Baptist.

Surprise me !

Since it literally means "messenger", Malachi could be a name, but equally it could be simply a title.

Simply... **the Apocrypha**

What is it?

The Apocrypha is the name given to Old Testament books found in some Bibles but not in others. These books come from an ancient translation of the Old Testament known as the Septuagint. This was a Greek translation made around 300 BC for the benefit of Jews living in Egypt who didn't speak Hebrew. The Septuagint has extra books as well as additional chapters to Esther, Daniel, Jeremiah, and Psalms. These books appear in some Bibles – those of the Catholic and Eastern Churches – but not in Jewish or modern Protestant Bibles.

The name comes from Jerome, who translated the Bible into Latin. He called them "Apocrypha", which means "hidden things".

1 Maccabees

1 Maccabees tells the story of the Maccabean wars, when the Jewish religion was under threat of destruction by Greek-speaking rulers. The Jews revolted against their rulers, led by a man called Judas Maccabeus (and others of his family). It also tells the story of the Jewish festival of Hanukkah. It was originally written in Hebrew, probably around 130–100 BC.

2 Maccabees

2 Maccabees is a summary of a lost, five-volume work by someone called Jason of Cyrene. It tells the story of the events that led up to the outbreak of revolt, and then reports the subsequent battles up to 161 BC. It was written sometime between 124 BC and the arrival of the Romans in 63 BC, and is mainly concerned with asserting the vital importance of the Temple and the Jewish Law. It's generally assumed to be less historically reliable than 1 Maccabees.

3 Maccabees

Greek Orthodox Bibles also include 3 Maccabees. This is an account of God's miraculous interventions on behalf of persecuted Jews in Alexandria, Egypt. It's got nothing to do with the Maccabees, since the events it details took place (a) fifty years before the Maccabean revolt and (b) in Egypt.

Esdras

1 Esdras is a retelling of various portions of Jewish history, drawing heavily on Chronicles and Ezra. ("Esdras" is the Greek form of the Hebrew name "Ezra".) 2 Esdras is a piece of apocalyptic writing trying to explain why God allowed the Romans to destroy the Jewish Temple in AD 70. It contains writings from different times and authors, some of which are later Christian interpolations.

Ecclesiasticus, aka The Wisdom of Ben Sirach

This is a wisdom book, a bit like Proverbs. It includes a famous passage that begins, "Let us now praise famous men" (Sirach 44:1 – 50:29), which not only mentions great heroes of the Old Testament but also includes the author himself! It was written around 200–180 BC.

The Book of Wisdom, aka The Wisdom of Solomon

A wisdom book which is a kind of positive reply to Ecclesiastes. It's the anti-Koheleth. It talks a lot about the uses of wisdom, particularly in preparing a soul for life after death. Since it was composed in Greek (and probably between 30 BC and AD 70), it's unlikely that Solomon had anything to do with it!

Tobit

Tobit tells the story of a Jew living in Nineveh. A devout, faithful blind man has his fortunes (and eyesight) restored through the actions of his son, Tobias, and the angel Raphael, disguised as a relative called Azariah. The book's message is that piety will be rewarded.

Judith

Judith is an Esther-like story of a Jewish woman living in Jerusalem when the city is under attack by the Assyrians. She sneaks into the enemy camp, seduces the Assyrian general, and cuts off his head, leading to an amazing victory. It was written by a Palestinian Jew with a very shaky grasp of history.

Others

As well as entire books, the Apocrypha also includes additions to existing books of the Old Testament.

There are four extra parts to the book of Daniel. There are additions to the story of the young men in the fiery furnace (The Prayer of Azariah). The story of Susanna is perhaps the earliest detective story in the world and tells how Daniel rescues a woman unjustly accused of adultery. Bel and the Dragon (which becomes the Greek Daniel chapter 14) tells how Daniel escapes from a plot to put him to death.

There are additions to the Book of Esther, which include a new prologue, Mordecai's dream, letters from the emperor, and various prayers.

The book of Baruch (who was Jeremiah's secretary) is an add-on to Jeremiah and contains a letter to the Jews in exile, as well as a prose prayer and two poems.

The Prayer of Manasseh apparently relates the prayer of King Manasseh who, after a lifetime of wickedness, repents of his sins before he dies.

Psalm 151 is an extra seven-verse psalm, celebrating David's defeat of Goliath.

Simply… **MATTHEW**

News for the Jews

What is it?

The life story of Yeshua (Jesus) of Nazareth. Matthew's Gospel has a very Jewish feel. It emphasizes the fulfilment of Old Testament prophecy, uses a lot of Jewish terminology, and contains more Old Testament quotes than any other Gospel. This Gospel aims to prove that Jesus is the messiah (which is why Matthew includes a family tree showing Jesus' descent from King David). But, although it is aimed at Jewish readers, Matthew's Gospel does not contain a narrow message. The kingdom is open to all, from whatever nation.

@

MATTHEW

Jesus is the messiah come to inaugurate the kingdom of heaven. It was predicted by the prophets and I've got tons of OT quotes to prove it!

Starring: Jesus, Mary and Joseph, wise men, King Herod, John the Baptist, disciples, Caiaphas, Pilate, Pharisees, etc.

What happens?

Matthew begins with Jesus' family tree. Mary conceives by the Holy Spirit. Jesus is born in Bethlehem. ❶ The family are visited by wise men. Herod massacres children in an attempt to kill Jesus, but the family escape to Egypt. They return after Herod's death, settling in Nazareth ❷.

Years pass. Jesus is baptized by John the Baptist, then tempted in the wilderness. He goes to Galilee, gathers disciples, and begins his work of healing and casting out demons. He announces good news for the poor ❸, and teaches about forgiveness, non-violence, and prayer ❹. He performs spectacular miracles – even bringing a girl back to life ❺. He feeds thousands of people. He walks on water. After Peter declares him to be the Christ (the anointed one of God), Jesus goes to a mountain where he appears in a shining light alongside Moses and Elijah ❻.

Jesus and his disciples head to Jerusalem, where Jesus enters the city in triumph and evicts the traders from the Temple ❼. Later that week, he shares a last supper with his disciples. But he is betrayed by Judas (who later commits suicide), arrested, and tried by the high priest, Caiaphas ❽. The next morning Jesus is taken to the Roman prefect, Pilate, who offers the crowd the choice of Jesus or a criminal called Barabbas. They reject Jesus. He is taken away and crucified. On his death there is an earthquake, tombs in the city open, and the curtain in the Temple is torn in two. The Jewish authorities ask for guards to be put on the tomb ❾.

After the Sabbath some women go to the tomb. The earth shakes and an angel rolls the stone away. The guards faint. The women meet the risen Jesus, who tells them to tell the disciples to meet him in Galilee. The Jewish leaders get the guards to spread rumours of tomb robbing. The eleven disciples go to Galilee, where they meet Jesus, who instructs them to tell all the world about him and make disciples ❿.

Why does it matter?

Matthew's Gospel contains much that is in the other synoptics – but also much unique material. He includes the famous sermon on the mount (chapters 5–7). He gives us longer teaching from Jesus on the end times and different details about the supernatural events at the time of Jesus' resurrection. The emphasis is on "the kingdom of heaven". Matthew ends with what is known as the great commission: Jesus' instruction to the disciples to go and spread the good news about him throughout the world.

IN TEN

❶ **Jesus' birth: 1:18 – 2:12**
❷ **Escape from Herod: 2:13–23**
❸ **Rules for discipleship: 4:18 – 5:11**
❹ **Radical teaching: 5:38–48; 6:9–15**
❺ **Spectacular miracles: 8:23 – 9:26**
❻ **Who am I?: 16:13–20**
❼ **The entry: 21:1–17**
❽ **Last evening: 26:17–68**
❾ **Death: 27:15–66**
❿ **Back to life: 28:1–20**

Surprise me

The sermon on the mount wasn't a sermon (and it wasn't much of a mount). The term was first applied by Augustine in the fourth century.

Simple truth about Jesus

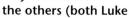

Starring: Jesus Christ, Peter and the other eleven disciples, Jewish religious leaders, Pilate, and John the Baptist

What is it?

It's "Jesus – The Intro", a brief, action-packed account of Jesus' life. The shortest of the Gospels, Mark was probably written before the others (both Luke and Matthew use large chunks of Mark), probably in the early AD 60s. The early church attributed it to John Mark, friend of Peter and Paul and nephew of Barnabas (Acts 12:12). Mark was probably writing mainly for a Gentile, Roman audience. He writes in a simple type of Greek, carefully explaining Jewish customs and translating Aramaic words and phrases.

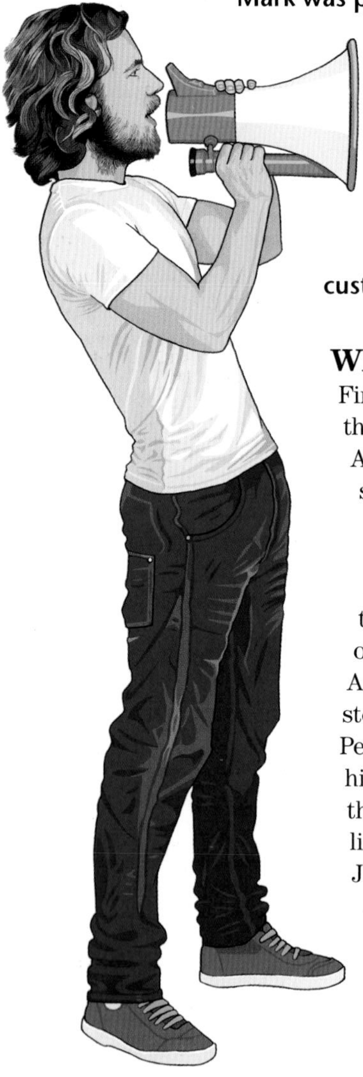

What happens?

First, John the Baptist announces the coming of Jesus; then Jesus is baptized and tempted in the wilderness ❶. After John is arrested, Jesus goes to Galilee and starts proclaiming the kingdom of God. He heals the sick, cleanses lepers, and casts out unclean spirits. His actions draw crowds and lead to opposition. Even his family try to stop him ❷. He teaches through parables – stories with meanings. He casts out demons. Then John is executed after Herod Antipas makes a drunken promise to his dancing-girl stepdaughter ❸. After a series of spectacular miracles Peter declares Jesus to be the messiah. But Jesus warns his disciples that he must suffer and die. He takes them up a mountain, where he appears in a shining light alongside Moses and Elijah ❹. Then it's off to Jerusalem. On the way Jesus slaps down arguments among his disciples about who is the greatest. In the kingdom of God, true greatness lies in serving others ❺.

Mark takes us through the last week. Day one: Jesus enters Jerusalem. Day two: he throws the money changers out of the Temple ❻. Day three: he answers questions in the Temple; then he foretells the Temple's fate under the Romans ❼. Day four: he is anointed with costly ointment at Bethany and that night Judas agrees to betray him ❽. Day five: it happens: Jesus shares Passover with his disciples, goes out to Gethsemane to pray, and is arrested. Day six: The Temple authorities take him to Pilate, who agrees to have him crucified ❾. He dies and is buried, but when the women go to the tomb a few days later, they find the tomb opened and empty. A young man in white tells them that Jesus has risen. His disciples are to go to Galilee and wait for him ❿.

Surprise me !

Mark's Gospel ends abruptly, with no resurrection appearance – just two women, an empty tomb, and an angel with a message from God. Although some versions of Mark include alternative, longer endings, these are later add-ons. The original ending is probably lost.

Why does it matter?

Mark ignores Jesus' birth. He opens with his core message: "The beginning of the good news of Jesus Christ, the Son of God." Mark reminds us that Jesus was a healer, an exorcist, a teacher, and someone who was passionately committed to the poor and the outcasts. It shows us a man modelling an entirely different kingdom: the kingdom of God, where the last are the first, where the leaders are slaves and servants. This is a place of healings and miracles but also suffering, hardship, and service.

IN TEN

10

❶ John the Baptist: 1:1–13
❷ Opposition: 3:1–35
❸ The death of John: 6:14–29
❹ True glory: 8:27 – 9:29
❺ Who wants to be great?: 10:35–45
❻ Entering Jerusalem: 11:1–33
❼ Not one stone will be left: 13:1–36
❽ Plots and perfume: 14:1–11
❾ Arrest and trial: 14:32 – 15:15
❿ Death and back again: 15:16 – 16:8

@

MARK

Jesus is the Son of God. He proves this through his miracles and by his death and resurrection. Welcome to the kingdom of God, everyone!

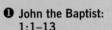

The case for Christ

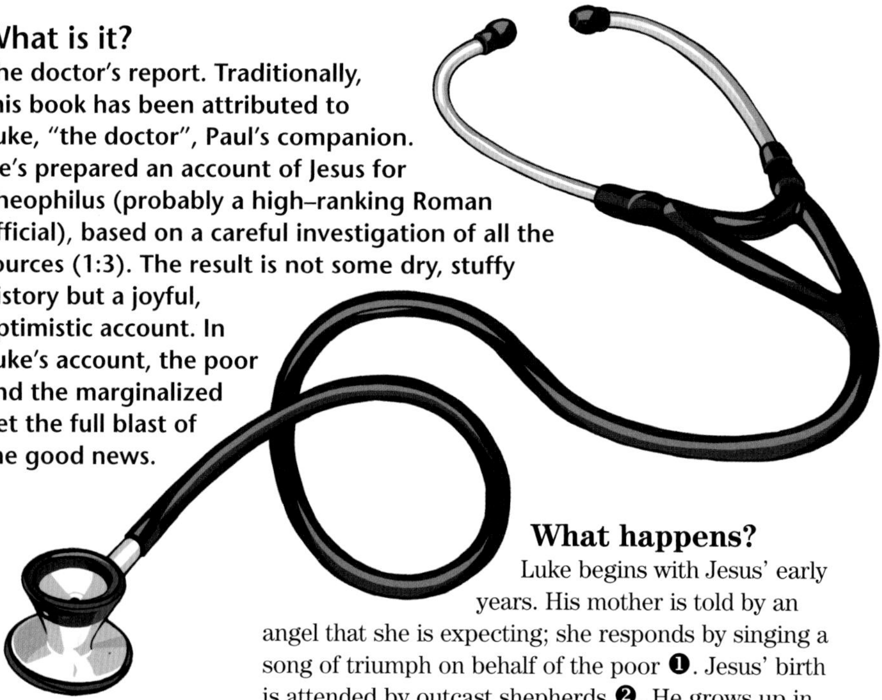

What is it?

The doctor's report. Traditionally, this book has been attributed to Luke, "the doctor", Paul's companion. He's prepared an account of Jesus for Theophilus (probably a high-ranking Roman official), based on a careful investigation of all the sources (1:3). The result is not some dry, stuffy history but a joyful, optimistic account. In Luke's account, the poor and the marginalized get the full blast of the good news.

What happens?

Luke begins with Jesus' early years. His mother is told by an angel that she is expecting; she responds by singing a song of triumph on behalf of the poor ❶. Jesus' birth is attended by outcast shepherds ❷. He grows up in Galilee (with the occasional adventure in Jerusalem) ❸.

Jesus is baptized by John the Baptist, and tempted in the wilderness. He goes to Nazareth, where his home town rejects him ❹. He moves to Capernaum where he recruits disciples to follow him. Outsiders, foreigners, and the marginalized are attracted to Jesus. A local centurion's slave is healed. A widow's son is brought back to life. Women, especially, are involved. He forgives a notorious "sinful woman" and his followers include women from Galilee ❺. His miracles and teaching attract attention. When Herod Antipas – the ruler of Galilee – hears of Jesus, he thinks he is

@ LUKE

`Have collected the stories, sifted the facts, arranged everything in order. Here's my report about Jesus. And it's good news for everyone.`

Starring: Jesus, John the Baptist, Mary, Joseph, the disciples, Herod Antipas, Pilate, the Temple leaders, plus supporting cast

Elijah or John the Baptist, back from the dead.

On the way to Jerusalem Jesus tells stories with unusual heroes: Samaritans, beggars invited to a banquet, lost sheep, prodigal sons ❻. In Jericho a despised tax collector is welcomed into the kingdom ❼. He enters Jerusalem in triumph, throws the traders out of the Temple, and teaches about the future. The Temple authorities plot to kill him. After sharing a last supper with his disciples Jesus is arrested and taken before the powers-that-be: the Temple authorities, Herod Antipas, and Pilate ❽. Jesus is crucified and dies. A Roman soldier recognizes who he really is ❾. A few days later women approach the tomb to find it open and empty. Two angels tell them that Jesus has risen. Outside the city, on the road to Emmaus, two travellers encounter the risen Jesus. Later, he appears to his disciples in the room where they are gathered. He tells them to stay there and wait to be given power from on high ❿.

IN TEN

❶ Good news for the poor: 1:1–56
❷ The birth: 2:1–21
❸ Youth and upbringing: 2:39–52
❹ Jesus back home: 3:23 – 4:30
❺ The women: 7:36 – 8:3
❻ Stories of the kingdom: 10:25–37; 15:11–32
❼ A tax collector: 19:1–10
❽ Arrest and trials: 22:47 – 23:25
❾ The death: 23:26–56
❿ The Emmaus road: 24:13–53

Why does it matter?

"He has brought down rulers from their thrones but has lifted up the humble," sings Mary, Jesus' mother. "He has filled the hungry with good things but has sent the rich away empty" (1:52–53). And that kind of sums up the Gospel of Luke. It's full of outsiders: tax collectors, prostitutes, lepers, and thieves. The news of Jesus' birth comes to humble, despised shepherds. There are Gentile heroes as well: centurions and Samaritans. This is the good news for all races. Like Matthew, Luke includes a genealogy, but his goes back to Adam, the father of all.

Surprise me

Luke's Gospel is the first part of a two-part work. He also wrote the book of Acts, which takes the story from the resurrection of Jesus through the spread of the early church.

Jesus from another perspective

What is it?

It's a reflective, not to say mysterious, account of Jesus' life. If it were a film it would have a lot of dry ice and voice-overs. John's Gospel is very different from the other three: there is a different structure entirely. In the other Gospels Jesus is in Galilee and then goes up to Jerusalem. But in John's Gospel he makes at least four visits to Jerusalem. Similarly, there is more interpretation and reflection. Not to mention some very long speeches.

Starring: John the Baptist, various disciples, Nicodemus, Lazarus, Mary and Martha, Mary Magdalene, Pilate and the high priests, and featuring, of course, Jesus as "the Word"

What happens?

The Gospel begins before the creation of the world: John claims Jesus was with God before creation as "the Word" ❶. After this cosmic opening we have John the Baptist proclaiming and identifying Jesus. Jesus' work kicks off with his first miracle – his first sign – at a wedding, where he turns water into wine ❷. After this, he visits Jerusalem, where he clears the traders out of the Temple. On this trip he meets Nicodemus the Pharisee ❸. After some time working alongside John, Jesus heads back to Galilee. There he performs some spectacular miracles: healings, walking on water, feeding 5,000 people. The crowd want to make him king, but he escapes ❹.

He makes claims about himself: he is the bread of life, the light of the world, the great "I am" (a clear claim to divinity) ❺. A later visit results in a riot which threatens his life, and he has to escape. But he goes back when he hears that his friend Lazarus is ill. When he gets to Bethany, he raises Lazarus from the dead ❻.

He returns to Jerusalem one final time. He enters in triumph. At the end of that week, he shares a meal

@ JOHN

Before creation Jesus (the "Word") was with God. He became flesh and lived on earth. Listen to his words. Look at his signs. Then believe!

Surprise me

Although the Gospel is traditionally attributed to John, the author is never identified. He simply describes himself as "the beloved disciple".

with his disciples during which he washes their feet as a sign that they must serve one another ❼. Then, in Gethsemane, he is arrested. He is tried before the high priests and the Roman prefect, Pilate. He is sentenced, flogged, and crucified ❽.

A few days later some women go and find the tomb empty. One of them, Mary Magdalene, sees a man she thinks is the gardener ❾. She discovers it is Jesus. He then appears to the other disciples, including Thomas, who initially doubted the stories. Finally, he appears to seven of his disciples on the shores of Lake Galilee ❿.

Why does it matter?

This is a gospel that explores who Jesus really is. Jesus, from the very start of John's Gospel, is much more than a human being; he is God, and he always has been. As proof, Jesus performs seven miraculous signs in John, each of which tells us more about his nature and origins. And there are seven "I am…" statements, which tell us more about Jesus' nature. So this is more than a record of what Jesus did: it's a powerful, deep reflection on *who* he is.

IN TEN

- ❶ **In the beginning: 1:1–18**
- ❷ **The wedding: 2:1–12**
- ❸ **Born again: 3:1–21**
- ❹ **Miraculous feeding and water walking: 6:1–21**
- ❺ **"I am… ": 6:22–59**
- ❻ **The raising of Lazarus: 11:1–44**
- ❼ **Washing feet: 13:1–20**
- ❽ **Jesus and Pilate: 19:1–30**
- ❾ **The gardener: 20:1–30**
- ❿ **Galilee: 21:1–24**

The early church in action

What is it?

It's Luke's report, part 2. The story of the early church, from the resurrection of Jesus in Jerusalem to the imprisonment of Paul in Rome (around AD 62). The traditional view is that this is the second book written by Luke the doctor, who also wrote the Gospel. Jesus promised his followers that he would send them the Holy Spirit. This book tells that story and what happens next. Luke had written an account of Jesus' life; now he tells the story of the early church.

@

ACTS

Jesus goes to heaven & his followers become Spirit-powered. This is what they did next: spreading out, changing lives, breaking boundaries.

IN TEN

10

1. The Holy Spirit: 2:1–47
2. Stephen's death: 6:8 – 8:3
3. Saul's conversion: 9:1–31
4. Clean and unclean: 10:1–48
5. The "Christians": 11:19–28
6. Council meeting: 15:1–35
7. Thessalonica to Athens: 17:1–34
8. God, not goddesses: 19:21–41
9. Paul's arrest: 21:17–36
10. Arrival in Rome: 28:16–30

What happens?

We start after the resurrection, with Jesus still appearing to his disciples. Then he goes out to the Mount of Olives and is taken "up" into heaven. But he promises them that someone else will come: a helper. The disciples are all together when the Holy Spirit descends on them ❶. Suddenly they start to speak out boldly, despite opposition from the authorities. The group of followers begins to grow. They appoint Greek-speaking Jews to help them look after everyone, and one of these, Stephen, is killed in Jerusalem. The action against them is organized by a man called Saul ❷. Saul starts to hunt down the followers of Jesus, but on his way to Damascus he has a vision of him. His whole life is turned around ❸.

Peter, meanwhile, has a vision in which God tells him that there is no longer any distinction between Jew

Starring: Jesus, Peter and the other disciples, Barnabas, Stephen, Philip, Cornelius, Paul of Tarsus, Priscilla and Aquila, Lydia and Luke, and introducing the Holy Spirit as himself

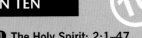

and Gentile ❹. As proof of this a centurion called Cornelius becomes a believer. The church grows. It spreads into Antioch in Syria, where the followers are first called Christians ❺. Saul joins that church and starts going on missionary journeys (during which he changes his name to Paul). But should Gentiles obey the Jewish Law? A council meeting in Jerusalem decides that they do not have to ❻. After this, Paul takes the gospel deep into Gentile territory. He plants churches in places such as Philippi and Thessalonica. In Athens he encounters philosophers ❼. In Ephesus he comes into conflict with the local cult of Artemis ❽.

In the end he returns to Jerusalem, where his presence causes a riot ❾. He spends two years under arrest in Caesarea before being shipped to Rome. On the way he suffers a shipwreck, but arrives there safely in the end ❿.

Why does it matter?

The early church grows at lightning speed. Along the way it has a lot of learning to do. What does it mean to follow Jesus? What should their relationship be with the Roman and Jewish authorities? Can Gentiles become Christians as well? Acts tells the history of the first decades of the church. But it is also a kind of biography of the Holy Spirit, who is a constant figure in the background, inspiring, protecting, punishing, informing, and pushing the first Christians to ever greater lengths as they spread the good news of Jesus Christ.

Surprise me !

Clearly it is the work of a companion of Paul – there are large chunks of the book where the writer uses the word "we", indicating that he was part of what was going on. This is eyewitness stuff.

Faith, among other things

What is it?

A revolutionary manifesto. Paul wrote this sometime in the spring of AD 57 when he was in Corinth. He was writing to a church he had never visited, but which included people whom he knew, and his reason was partly to introduce himself in anticipation of a visit. But the letter sums up one of his great theories: salvation by grace through faith. This powerful idea has repeatedly fuelled reform and renewal of the church across the centuries.

@ **ROMANS**

`Good news! We are saved by grace through faith. Now we must live as children of God, in the hope of future glory. PS: See you soon in Rome!`

Starring: Paul, Tertius (his secretary), Timothy, the church in Rome including Prisca and Aquila, Andronicus, Junias, and a whole load of others

What happens?

From Paul, an apostle ❶. The power of the gospel means the righteous will live by faith ❷. No one is without guilt; all have sinned ❸. But the good news is that through faith we can be saved ❹. Through the sacrifice of Jesus, we can live a new life ❺.

This doesn't mean that we can just go on sinning. Just the opposite: we must obey Jesus and live for him ❻. Life in the Spirit is a life

without condemnation, empowered by the Spirit of God. If we are led by the Spirit, then we are children of God ❼. The goal is future glory as resurrected beings. The entire creation waits to be set free, transformed. This gives us hope and confidence, for nothing can separate us from the love of Christ ❽. Salvation is for all – including the Israelites, God's chosen people.

We are not to be like the world, but transformed into a different kind of being, a body of people, all with different gifts but loving, serving, hoping, rejoicing, and persevering ❾. We are not to be judgmental, not to quarrel, not to do things that cause others to stumble.

Paul feels able to write to them boldly because of his track record. And he intends to visit them soon ❿. The letter ends with greetings to the church and a final instruction to avoid dissension.

IN TEN

❶ **Paul the apostle: 1:1–15**
❷ **Good news: 1:16–17**
❸ **No one is good: 3:1–20**
❹ **Great news: 3:21–31**
❺ **New life: 5:1–11**
❻ **In Christ: 6:1–23**
❼ **Live through the Spirit: 8:1–17**
❽ **The future: 8:18–39**
❾ **New life: 12:1–21**
❿ **Bold writing: 15:14–33**

Why does it matter?

Romans is one of the most important documents ever written. After reading this, Martin Luther put in motion the ideas behind the Reformation, which have crucially shaped the modern world. We are not saved because of what we do, but through faith in Jesus: that's the golden thread that runs right through Romans. This is a fundamental message of freedom. But we should also remember that the last four chapters of Romans are full of practical stuff about how Christians are supposed to live Christ-shaped lives of love, peace, and hope. But this is a response to salvation, not what we do in order to obtain it.

Surprise me

In the New Testament, Romans is the first of Paul's letters, not because he wrote it before the others but because it is the longest.

The greatest thing is love

What is it?

It's a threatening letter. A correction. A "must-do-better" report. Paul is writing to the Christians in Corinth, an important, cosmopolitan port city about forty miles south-west of Athens. He is writing around AD 55 from Ephesus. He has helped to establish the church in Corinth some three years earlier, but things have gone wrong. There is serious sexual sin in the church, not to mention schisms and elitist behaviour all too typical of the wealthy, worldly society of Corinth.

Starring: Paul, Apollos and Cephas [Peter], plus Chloë, Gaius, Stephanas, and various unruly members of the Corinthian church

IN TEN

❶ Gang warfare: 1:10–31
❷ Grow up!: 3:1–23
❸ Sexual immorality: 5:1–13
❹ A slave for everyone: 9:1–27
❺ Rules for worship: 11:1–34
❻ One body: 12:1–31
❼ Love: 13:1–13
❽ Help each other: 14:1–25
❾ We will be raised: 15:1–34
❿ Death is dead: 15:35–58

What happens?

From "Paul, called to be an apostle of Christ... ". There are quarrels in the Corinthian church and "gangs", some of which are questioning Paul's abilities and credentials ❶. Paul reminds them of his status and of how the church was formed from humble, "foolish" people. They are to stop acting so childishly, because everyone belongs to Christ ❷. There is also a serious case of sexual immorality in the church ❸, and even lawsuits between believers. Paul gives a series of instructions concerning the way that believers should act and relate to one another. He addresses questions about his own apostleship and behaviour. He has made himself a slave to everyone, all for the sake of the gospel ❹. The behaviour of the Corinthian church has infected their worship and, especially, their observance of the Lord's Supper, in which the rich are humiliating the poor. Paul points out what he has learned and instructs them to behave properly ❺. Some members are priding themselves on their spiritual gifts. Paul reminds them that they are one body; they all have different gifts ❻. He urges them to pursue the greatest gift – love ❼. The point of worship is to demonstrate not division but unity; to build one another up ❽. Finally, Paul restates the fundamental truth: Christ died for their sins and was resurrected ❾. Like him, they know that the believer's destiny is to be raised from the dead. Death has been defeated ❿.

@ 1CORINTHIANS

Factions? Sexual sin? Lawsuits? Selfishness? Grow up! We're all one body. Don't care how "spiritual" you are; without love it means nothing.

Why does it matter?

The Corinthian church were behaving just like the society around them. They were infected with snobbery and elitism and tainted with serious sexual sin. Their worship was both a shambles and a sham. They were behaving like spoilt brats, rather than children of God. So Paul calls on them to grow up and stop arguing. Above all, he talks about love. In one of the greatest pieces of prose ever written he argues that love is the most important thing (chapter 13).

If they only loved one another, then the splits and the arguments would disappear.

Surprise me !

Although this is called "1 Corinthians" it is not the first letter that Paul wrote to this church. He is following up a previous letter, which we no longer have (5:9).

Jars of clay

What is it?

A making-up note. A reconciliation. Paul has now left Ephesus, but before then he has visited Corinth on a trip that proved to be extremely painful. But now he hears that his words have had some effect. The Corinthian church have changed their ways. And yet there are still grumbles. Paul had promised to return, but has decided that another painful visit would serve no purpose. His opponents now claim that Paul doesn't keep his promises. He is forced to defend his conduct and his work for the gospel. The result is one of his most personal, poignant letters.

@ **2CORINTHIANS**
We are God-powered people. We're afflicted, persecuted, weighed down, and attacked. But we never give up, never despair, never lose heart.

What happens?

Paul is with Timothy. He tells the Corinthians about the sufferings he experienced in Ephesus and his escape from "a deadly peril". He justifies his decision not to visit Corinth again: he is not breaking a promise; he is sparing them further pain ❶. Now he has heard that things have changed in Corinth, and this fills him with hope and confidence.

Though Christians are like jars of clay, they have an imperishable treasure inside them. They are afflicted but not crushed; persecuted but not destroyed; knocked down but undefeated. They don't lose heart ❷. Paul is full of joy at the news of repentance from Corinth. He has been worried and sad, but now he is rejoicing ❸. He encourages the church to give

Starring: Paul, Timothy, Titus, and those Christians at Corinth again

generously to the collection he is organizing for the church in Judea. Then he switches tack and starts to defend his own ministry. Unimpressive in person, lacking the famous Greek eloquence and rhetoric, his boast is in the Lord ❹. He challenges the false apostles who have caused such damage. Do they have a track record to challenge his? Have they faced beatings and imprisonment, shipwrecks, danger from bandits, hunger, cold, and anxiety? Have they seen the same visions he has? ❺ Paul writes that he will visit them again. And he hopes then to find them as he would wish.

IN FIVE

- ❶ Non-arrival: 1:1 – 2:17
- ❷ Jars of clay: 4:1–18
- ❸ Light and dark: 6:14 – 7:16
- ❹ A true apostle: 10:1–18
- ❺ An apostle's sufferings: 11:16 – 12:10

Why does it matter?

In 2 Corinthians, Paul gives us a vivid impression of the cost of discipleship. He defends his apostleship by listing all that he has had to endure. Imprisonment, beatings, shipwrecks, unrelenting danger – no mega churches and big worship bands here! And the strain is mental as well as physical: it's impossible not to feel the weight of Paul's anxiety for the Corinthian church. But, in all this, it is God's strength that shines through. God's grace is sufficient; his power is made perfect in weakness. We are jars of clay, but the imperishable, indestructible, inexhaustible power inside us comes from God.

Surprise me

Again, we're missing a letter. Paul seems to have sent a harsh letter between 1 Corinthians and 2 Corinthians, although some people believe that harsh letter might be preserved here as chapters 10–13.

Freedom!

Starring: Paul, Barnabas, Cephas [Peter], and the "Judaizers"

What is it?

This is a wonderful, eloquent rant. It's grievous bodily theology. Passionate, angry, entertainingly outspoken, Paul responds to claims that the Gentile converts he made in Galatia on his first journey must be circumcised and live as Jews. (At one point he suggests that those who suggest others should be circumcised should cut the whole lot off!) Paul is in Antioch, where the same kind of people have forced a split between Paul and Peter and Barnabas. Unity has been shattered. This is not what Paul has been working for. And he lets them all know – Peter, his opponents, the Galatians – everyone gets it. Full blast.

@ GALATIANS

We are free! So don't allow anyone to enslave you to old rules. Live by the Spirit and bear good fruit (& if you don't like it, tough!).

What happens?

Paul's status as an apostle comes not from humans, but from Jesus Christ. Once he persecuted the church; now he proclaims the truth ❶. He shares his personal biography and then talks about the situation in Antioch, where Cephas [Peter] and Barnabas have even been persuaded not to eat with the Gentile Christians, for fear of impurity. Paul himself challenges Peter on his behaviour ❷.

Paul berates the Galatians for being foolish and

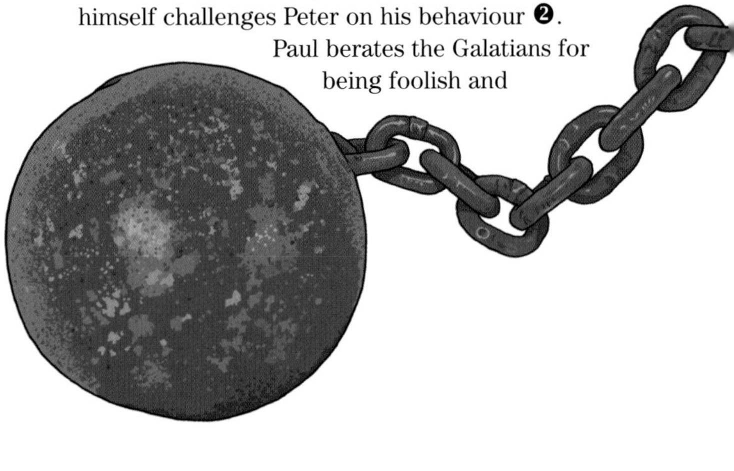

"bewitched". They should remember that the righteous will live by faith ❸. Amazingly, he says that there is no longer any difference between Jew and Gentile, slave and free, male and female: all are one in Jesus Christ. We are all children of God ❹. Jesus has set us free. But freedom does not mean that we can do what we like. Instead, we must live by the Spirit, not by the desires of the flesh. We must be guided by the Spirit, and then our lives will bear fruit: love, joy, peace, patience, kindness, generosity, faithfulness, gentleness, self-control. Neither being circumcised nor being uncircumcised matters, but being a new creation is everything ❺.

IN FIVE

❶ A true apostle: 1:1–24
❷ A bit of biography: 2:1–21
❸ Foolish people!: 3:1–14
❹ No difference: 3:23 – 4:7
❺ True freedom: 5:1 – 6:10

Why does it matter?

This is a passionate argument for freedom. The Galatians have been set free by Christ; now others want to enslave them to the Law. But Paul says it's no longer required. The ancient world was very aware of class, gender, and status. But, in one of the most radical statements in ancient history, Paul argues that there is no longer any difference between Jew and Gentile, slave and free, male and female: all are one in Jesus Christ. To the orthodox Jews who thought all Gentiles impure, it would have been heresy. But, Paul says, Jesus Christ has changed everything.

Surprise me

Paul went to Galatia in around AD 48. If this letter was written soon afterwards, that makes it one of the earliest New Testament documents.

Let's stick together

What is it?

It's a circular letter. A bit like those ones you get at Christmas, only with more depth! The letter brings together some of the major themes of Paul's teaching, as a kind of summary of his thoughts. For that reason it's been suggested that the letter may have been intended as a general letter to several churches: this would explain its general nature and also the fact that it lacks any personal greetings.

@ EPHESIANS

We have been saved. We were dead in sin but now we're alive in Christ. So give up the old ways. Join together in unity and start to shine!

IN FIVE

❶ Destiny: 1:1–14
❷ The household of God: 2:11–22
❸ New life: 4:1–24
❹ Living for God: 5:6–20
❺ The fight: 6:10–24

Starring: Paul and Tychicus

What happens?

We have been chosen: that's the starting point. We are destined for adoption as children of God ❶. Paul gives thanks for the example of the Ephesians. As Gentiles they were dead in sin, living in the flesh, but they have been saved by the grace of God, prepared for a different way of life, brought from far off into the household of God ❷. That's why Paul is in prison: because of his desire to speak to the Gentile world. And as a prisoner he begs them to live in unity. Each person has different gifts, but we are one body, joined together. So no more living the old, futile Gentile life: instead, obey a new set of rules ❸. Speak the truth. Control your anger. Give up evil, sinful behaviour and wicked talk. Renounce those pagan ways ❹. Paul gives instructions for husbands, wives, and families. Then he advises his listeners to arm themselves for the fight. They are to wear the armour of God and to pray constantly, especially for Paul, their ambassador in chains ❺.

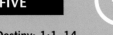

Surprise me

Ephesus was home to the Temple of Artemis – one of the seven wonders of the ancient world and a centre of pagan magic and the occult. This helps explain Paul's emphasis on the need for followers of Jesus to "have nothing to do with the fruitless deeds of darkness".

Why does it matter?

Christ is our peace. The walls of hatred between Jew and Gentile have been broken down. Followers of Jesus need to recognize that we are all joined together and that we should all work for and support one another. No one is more important than another. But we have to give up the old ways of life. No more living in the pagan style. Paul has an almost breathless tone of wonder at God's kindness, wisdom, and love. But he also talks about matter-of-fact things: controlling your tongue and your temper; asking for God's protection against evil. Avoid darkness, walk in the light.

Eyes on the prize

What is it?

It's a thank-you letter. The church at Philippi had sent Paul a gift, to support him while he was in prison (probably in Rome). Paul writes to thank them, but also to encourage them and to warn them about possible pitfalls. The Philippian church was always very special to Paul. He founded it around AD 50 on his second missionary journey and it had always supported him. So this is a very affectionate letter.

@ **PHILIPPIANS**

Thanks for the gift! I always think of you with joy. Keep running the race; there's a prize waiting for us all.

Starring: Paul, Timothy, Epaphroditus, Euodia, and Syntyche

What happens?

Paul begins with thanks: every time he remembers the Philippians he gives thanks because they have always shared with him in the work of the gospel. He prays that they would have more love, knowledge and insight, and produce a fine "harvest" ❶. His imprisonment, he argues, is a good thing in that it has furthered the gospel. He doesn't know how things will turn out, but he doesn't fear death ❷. He urges the Philippians to stand firm and to serve one another like Christ. He cites an early-church hymn which talks of how Jesus became a slave to serve others and was therefore exalted above all others ❸. He talks of sending Timothy to them, and he will send Epaphroditus, one of their own, who has been seriously ill. He reminds them that their righteousness comes from faith in Christ. They should press on, keep on running the race, like athletes running for a prize ❹. Finally, he urges two church members to make peace with each other. Rejoice always, he tells them. Remember what is true, pure, and honourable. And he ends as he begins, with thanks for their care and concern and memories of the ways in which they have always stood by him ❺.

IN FIVE

❶ Paul's prayer: 1:1–11
❷ No fear: 1:12–30
❸ True humility: 2:1–18
❹ Run the race: 3:1–21
❺ Final thanks: 4:10–23

Surprise me

The first convert in Philippi was a woman called Lydia, and women continued to play a significant role in the church: Paul encourages two of them – Euodia and Syntyche – to be reconciled to each other (4:2).

Why does it matter?

"Keep on going": that's one of the key messages of Philippians. Paul is in prison when he writes this letter, and he is prepared to face that ordeal to the end. He doesn't want to die; he feels he still has work to do, but he is fully prepared to die. It's a letter full of encouragement. It also contains one of the greatest – and earliest – statements of faith, a very early Christian hymn or poem, which summarizes what Jesus did for us and how God has therefore raised him "above every name" (2:6–11).

Don't be fooled

What is it?

It's a rule clarification. Health and safety advice mixed with a thank-you letter. In jail, Paul meets Epaphras, the founder of the church at Colossae (as well as of churches in Laodicea and Hierapolis). The Colossians seem to have been lured into following a pick'n'mix selection of Jewish dietary laws, angel worship, and pagan new-moon festivals. Paul writes to encourage them to free themselves from such snares.

Starring: Paul, Epaphras, Tychicus, Onesimus, and Aristarchus

@

COLOSSIANS

Jesus is the supreme power, the image of God. Forget all those angels, powers, festivals, and food laws. Concentrate on him. He's all you need.

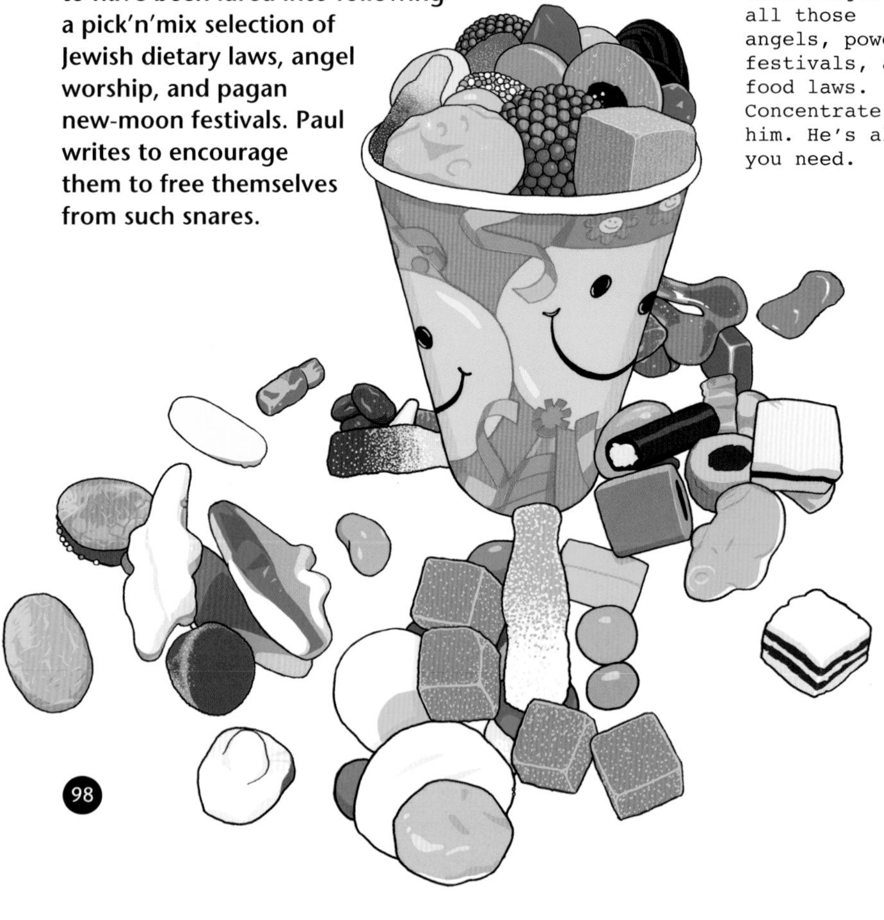

What happens?

Paul begins by giving thanks for the Colossian church. He has been told about them by Epaphras, the founder of this church. Paul prays that the church members may live lives worthy of Christ ❶. Jesus is supreme, the image of the invisible God. His death has made it possible for us to be presented to God as blameless and irreproachable. Paul talks about his struggles and suffering, which are not only on behalf of those he has met, but also for churches such as those at Colossae and Laodicea ❷. He urges them to make sure they are not deceived by false teaching. Nobody should condemn them on the basis of foolish theories, bizarre mysticism, or outmoded Jewish laws ❸. Instead, they have been raised to new life. So they should put away the old ways of living – the lies and idolatry and evil passions – and remember that as God's chosen ones they should live together in love ❹. He gives rules for family and domestic life before some final instructions: devote yourself to prayer; conduct yourself wisely; remember Paul in his chains. Oh, and pass this letter on to the Laodiceans ❺.

Why does it matter?

The big message here is the supremacy of Christ. Never mind all those angels and powers and strange ideas, Christ is the true image of God, the ruler of all of them. He has disarmed all those powers, rulers, and authorities: rooting our lives in him is all we need.

IN FIVE

5

- ❶ **Hello, Colossae: 1:1–8**
- ❷ **All about Jesus: 1:9 – 2:5**
- ❸ **Don't let them tell you what to do: 2:6–23**
- ❹ **New life in Christ: 3:1–17**
- ❺ **Pass it on: 4:2–18**

Surprise me !

This letter was intended to be read to another church. Paul gives instructions to pass it on to the church in Laodicea. Paul probably wrote this letter at the same time as Philemon and Ephesians: all three letters were sent with Paul's helpers Tychicus and Onesimus.

The return of the king

What is it?

It's like a quiet chat with Dad. Or Mum. Or an older brother. Paul set up the church in Thessalonica some time around AD 50. Because of fierce opposition he had to leave the city in a hurry, but he feels responsible for and proud of the church. He likens himself to a nursing mother or a father and his children. Some fourteen times he refers to the Thessalonian Christians as his brothers and sisters. He's writing to them to address two main issues: when the Lord will return and what to do while waiting.

@

1THESSALONIANS

I long to see you, but I can't. So stay strong. Keep going. And when Jesus comes back the dead will rise, and one day we will all be with him.

What happens?

Paul begins with a greeting from him and his team, Silas and Timothy. He gives thanks for the example of the Thessalonians: their willingness to respond to the gospel and to imitate the behaviour of the Lord ❶.

Starring: Paul, Silas, and Timothy

He recounts some of his work in the city: how he laboured to preach the gospel in spite of opposition and at no charge or cost to anyone ❷. When he was forced to leave the city, he felt as if he were orphaned. He wanted to return to Thessalonica but couldn't, so he sent Timothy back to strengthen and encourage them. Timothy has since returned to Paul with news of their faith and love ❸. Paul urges them to continue living a life pleasing to God. He then answers their questions about the future. Jesus will return and the dead will rise and the believers will be with the Lord for ever. No one knows when this will happen, so everyone must stay alert ❹. Finally, Paul urges the Thessalonians to respect their leaders and to persevere: rejoice always, pray continually, give thanks in all circumstances, hold fast ❺.

IN FIVE

- ❶ **Their faith: 1:1–10**
- ❷ **Paul's work: 2:1–20**
- ❸ **Orphaned: 2:17 – 3:13**
- ❹ **The Lord's return: 4:13 – 5:11**
- ❺ **Final instructions: 5:12–28**

Surprise me

The Greek word Paul uses to describe Jesus' return is *parousia*. This means "presence" and was usually used of the visit of someone such as the emperor to a city.

Why does it matter?

Paul has obviously developed a deep affection for the Christians at Thessalonica. He's full of joy at their efforts. But the key message here is about those of their number who have died before the Lord has returned. Paul says that they are not lost or gone for ever. The Lord is coming again and the dead will rise first and then we will all be with the Lord for ever.

And in the end...

What is it?

A follow-up to 1 Thessalonians. The church in Thessalonica is continuing to obsess about the return of Jesus – some are claiming that it has already happened and they have missed it – so Paul writes a further letter to give more information.

@ **2THESSALONIANS**
The day of the Lord is coming. But not yet. So get back to work.

Starring: Paul, Silas, and Timothy

What happens?

Paul begins by giving thanks for the Thessalonian church and commending their faith and perseverance. He recognises that they are undergoing persecution and affliction. He says that those who are attacking them will be punished. He goes on to talk about the day of judgment when Jesus will return ❶. He warns

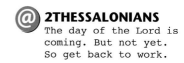

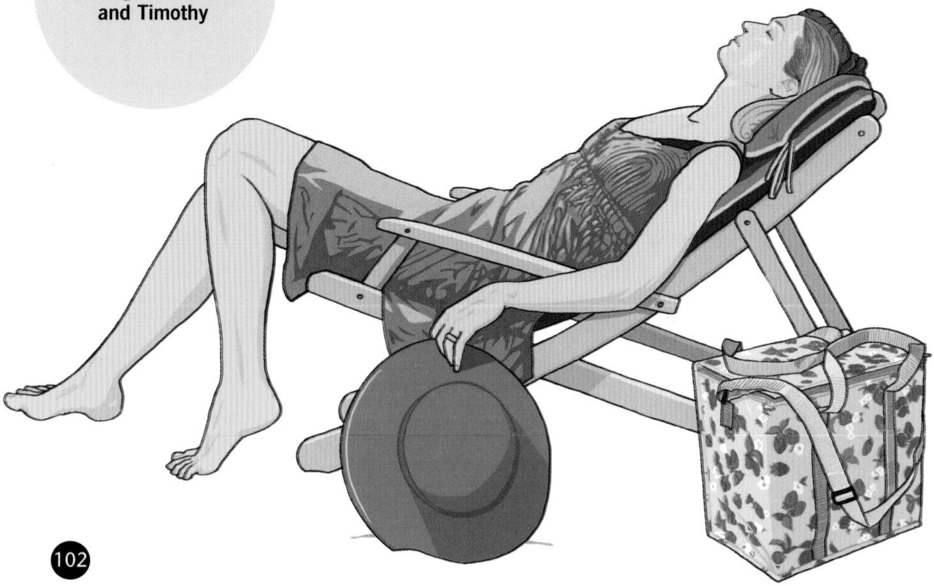

the Thessalonian Christians not to be deceived. Some are claiming that Paul has said that the day of the Lord has already arrived. Paul says that before that day there will come rebellion and someone called "the man of lawlessness". This being will oppose God and even claim to be God. At the moment this figure is being restrained, but he will arrive, and then he will be defeated by Jesus ❷.

Paul gives thanks again for the Thessalonian church who, he says, have been "chosen" – called through Paul's message of good news. He urges them to stand firmly by what he has taught them and prays that God will comfort and strengthen them. Finally, he asks them to pray for him. Some believers are living in idleness, not contributing to the community. Paul points to his own example while he was living with them: how he worked hard so as not to be a burden to them. Paul commands them to do their work quietly and earn their own living ❸. He signs the letter in his own hand as a guarantee of its authenticity.

IN THREE

- ❶ **The Lord will bring justice: 1:1–12**
- ❷ **The man of lawlessness: 2:1–12**
- ❸ **Be faithful and keep praying: 3:1–18**

Surprise me

Someone has been impersonating Paul. He talks about a letter that was "supposed to have come from us" (2:2).

Why does it matter?

The letter encourages the Thessalonian church to keep going. Although it contains information about "the end times", the real message is to keep going, imitating the Lord Jesus. He will arrive one day, so be prepared.

Fight the good fight

What is it?

It's a manual for church leadership. A master's tips to his apprentice. Paul regards Timothy as a "son". Timothy is now at Ephesus, helping to lead the church there. Paul writes to him giving guidelines on how to choose church leaders and how to combat false teaching.

Starring: Paul and Timothy

What happens?

Paul starts with a warning against false teaching. He has left Timothy in Ephesus in order to correct some of the myths, speculations, and meaningless talk which have been occupying them. There are people who want to be teachers of the law, without any real understanding. Paul recounts his own history and how Christ had mercy on him, even though he had been a violent persecutor ❶. He gives Timothy a series of instructions. He urges that prayer should be offered for everyone whatever their social status ❷; he gives advice on who should be allowed to teach and on the behaviour

@ 1TIMOTHY

Don't let others look down on you because you're young. Remember the promises. Remember what you must do. And don't get distracted by money.

of men and women. He lists the appropriate qualities for church leaders. They should be respectable, hospitable, good managers of their own households. They should be mature Christians, rather than recent converts ❸.

Then he talks about the qualities needed by Timothy himself. He tells Timothy not to let others despise him because of his youth; instead Timothy should set them an example of proper Christian behaviour. He urges Timothy to keep up the public reading and teaching of scripture. Above all, he should remember the prophecies that were given to him and the gifts which these prophecies confirmed ❹. He is to respect elders, look after widows, and keep himself pure. If we have food to eat and clothes to wear we should be content. The love of money is the root of all evil and has lured some away from the right path. Timothy is urged to stand firm, fight the good fight, and guard what has been entrusted to him. There are those in the church who are rich, but it is better for them to be rich in good works, and to be generous with their wealth. Compared to worldly wealth, that is true riches ❺.

IN FIVE

❶ False and true teaching: 1:1–20
❷ How to pray: 2:1–15
❸ Church leaders: 3:1–13
❹ Instructions: 4:6–16
❺ True wealth: 6:3–21

Surprise me

Paul tells Timothy that he should take a little wine for the sake of his stomach. The reason is that most water in the ancient world was impure: adding wine actually made it safer to drink.

Why does it matter?

Paul's overriding point is that Christians – and especially those in any position of leadership – have to embody lifestyles that reflect, not contradict, the gospel. Timothy is reminded of the basics: trust scripture, remember his calling, do the stuff he knows he should do. Leadership is not about age, status, wealth, or social position: it's about modelling the Christ-like life.

Hold on

What is it?

It's a cry from the heart. At times, almost a goodbye note. This letter from jail reveals the extent of Paul's commitment to the gospel. Paul is in prison in Rome. He writes to ask Timothy to join him – and also to encourage his protégé to persevere.

IN THREE

❶ No shame: 1:1–18
❷ Do your duty: 2:1–26
❸ Keep running: 3:10 – 4:8

What happens?

Starring: Paul, Timothy, Crescens, Titus, Tychicus, and Luke. And featuring Philetus, Hymenaeus, and Demas and Alexander the metalworker as "the baddies"

The memory of Timothy (and his mother, Eunice, and grandmother, Lois) brings Paul joy. He urges Timothy not to be ashamed of the gospel, but to join Paul in his sufferings. Paul has been abandoned by many, although Onesiphorus is not "ashamed" of Paul's chains ❶. Paul's gospel is Jesus Christ, raised from the dead: that's why he's chained like a criminal. He warns against wasting time on useless theological debate or stupid controversies. Stay focused: pursue righteousness, faith, love, and peace ❷. Paul talks about the many kinds of evil behaviour Timothy can expect to witness in the last days. Timothy must persist in proclaiming the gospel. But Paul feels that he is being poured out; he has finished his race, kept the faith ❸. He asks Timothy to come to him in Rome and bring some things from Troas. At his first defence, all his supporters have deserted him. His other friends are scattered. Only Luke is with him. Paul ends with a plaintive request: do your best to come before winter.

@

2TIMOTHY

Never be ashamed of the gospel. Everyone's left me. I feel as if it's all over. But I have run my race. Stay focused. Come to me if you can.

Surprise me

Along with some important books and parchments, Timothy is asked to bring Paul a cloak, which he has left in Troas. Winter is coming.

Why does it matter?

Paul is under no illusions: this could be the end. But he sees the bigger picture. "If we died with him, we will also live with him; if we endure, we will also reign with him… " (2:11–12). And he reminds his "son" of how Timothy has been specially commissioned for the work he is to do. He urges Timothy to hold on to sound teaching, to study the scriptures, and to keep on running the race.

Leadership matters

What is it?

It's one of those documentaries in which an expert goes in to try to turn a failing business around. Titus is Paul's troubleshooter, his go-to man, when he needs a problem solved or when he needs a "volunteer" to go into a tough situation. Paul advises Titus on leadership, holiness, and honesty.

Starring: Paul, Titus, Artemas, Tychicus, Zenas the lawyer, and Apollos

@ **TITUS**

The job in Crete would be easy if it weren't for Cretans. Appoint good leaders. Teach sound doctrine. Do the right stuff. Meet me in Nicopolis.

What happens?

Titus has been left in Crete by Paul to put the churches there in order and to appoint leaders ❶. Titus is to teach sound doctrine, and Paul gives him advice on how to deal with different groups of people: older men and women; young men; slaves ❷. They are all subject to rulers and authorities, and all should be ready to do good, to speak evil of no one, and to be gentle. Paul describes his previous existence, emphasizing how the goodness and kindness of Christ have saved him. Justified through

grace, we have the hope of eternal life. So we are to avoid pointless speculation and stupid quarrels, and deal firmly with those who cause division. Finally, Paul will send Artemas or Tychicus to Crete. He wants Titus to join him in Nicopolis ❸.

IN THREE

❶ Church leaders: 1:1–16
❷ Good examples: 2:1–15
❸ Doing good: 3:1–15

Why does it matter?

This letter gives an insight into the world of the early church and the qualities required of their leaders. Church leaders should be people of good reputation and personal behaviour. Arguments and disputes should be avoided. But upright lives are not just the work of leaders: all Christians have a duty, young and old, slave and free (2:1–10; 3:1–3). We used to be evil and stupid and disobedient, but that behaviour should have gone now. We have been given new life through Jesus, and that means new ways of behaving.

Surprise me

Paul is quite harsh about the Cretans. He quotes one of their own philosophers, who says, "Cretans are always liars, evil brutes, lazy gluttons" (1:12). Of course, logically that means the philosopher was himself lying, which means that this is a paradox.

No longer a slave

PHILEMON
Sending Onesimus back to you. No longer a slave, but a brother. If he owes you anything, charge it to me. And get the spare room ready.

What is it?

An email. Well, a personal note. It's not about doctrine, or about deep teaching. It's a request for reconciliation between a Christian slave and his Christian master. There was a problem between Onesimus and his boss. Some money or expense seems to have been involved. Something has caused Philemon to believe that Onesimus was "useless" (chapter 11). But Paul writes pleading that the two should be reconciled.

What happens?

Paul sends greetings to Philemon and the church that meets in his house. He thanks God for Philemon's faith and love. This gives him boldness to appeal to him. Paul is an old man, and he is writing on behalf of Onesimus, whom he views as a son. He is returning Onesimus to Philemon; he would like to keep him, but he thinks it better to send him back to Philemon. He urges Philemon to treat Onesimus as a brother, rather than as a slave. If Onesimus owes him anything, Philemon is to charge it to Paul. He hopes to be able to join Philemon in time. Others, including Epaphras, Mark, Aristarchus, and Luke, send their greetings ❶.

Starring: Paul, Philemon and Onesimus, and featuring Apphia, Archippus, Epaphras, Aristarchus, Demas, Mark, and Luke

IN ONE

❶ The same as me: 1–25

Surprise me

Paul refers to himself as "an old man" (chapter 10). The Greek word is *presbuteros*, which implies a man aged about sixty. Since this letter was written in the early AD 60s, this means that Paul was actually a contemporary of Jesus.

Why does it matter?

It is usually suggested that Onesimus is a runaway slave who has stolen some money. But that's never stated in the letter. (The idea that Onesimus was on the run wasn't suggested until three hundred years after the letter was originally written.) Whatever the case, Paul's request that Onesimus should be welcomed back "no longer as a slave, but better than a slave, as a dear brother" (chapters 15–16) would have been astonishingly radical in the first century. But Onesimus and Philemon are in the kingdom of God, where everyone is equal.

Faith and history

@ HEBREWS

Jesus is the new high priest and the once-for-all sacrifice. By faith we are sure of things hoped for and convinced of things not seen.

What is it?

It's the closest thing in the New Testament to a sermon. This is an in-depth interpretation of Jewish history and religious symbolism to show that Christ is the one that everyone has been waiting for. It was probably written to Jewish Christians in Rome. (Certainly it was written before the destruction of the Temple in Jerusalem in AD 70.)

What happens?

In the past God spoke to us through the prophets: today he speaks through his Son. For a while Jesus was lower than the angels, but now he is their superior. He became a man in order to save humanity ❶. Jesus is greater than Moses. He is a holy, blameless, eternal high priest ❷. Previous priests were of the old covenant, but now there is a new covenant, which makes the old one obsolete ❸.

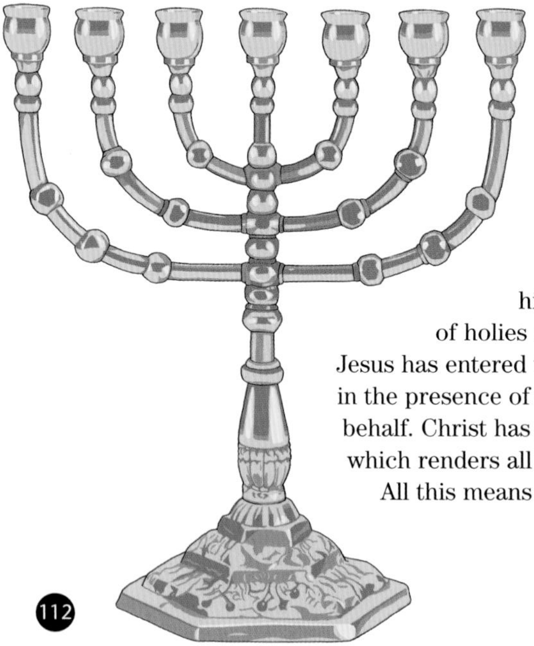

Under the old covenant, the high priest could only enter the holy of holies in the Temple once a year. But Jesus has entered the *real* holy of holies – appearing in the presence of God himself to intercede on our behalf. Christ has made the one great sacrifice, which renders all those other sacrifices obsolete.

All this means that we can confidently enter the

Starring: Jesus, Moses, Melchizedek, Abel, Enoch, Noah, and Abraham, and introducing [UNKNOWN] as the author

presence of God, through the sacrifice of Jesus and by "a new and living way" ❹.

We are people of faith. The author lists heroes of faith from Abel onwards, through Abraham, Moses, Rahab, and David – a great "cloud of witnesses". We should learn from their example: run the race and imitate Jesus ❺. He ends with a series of instructions: pursue peace and holiness; love one another; show hospitality; remember those in prison; honour marriage; don't love money; obey your leaders. Keep on doing good and sharing what you have: that's the sacrifice that pleases God.

IN FIVE

5

- ❶ Tempted as we were: 2:5–18
- ❷ Great high priest: 4:14 – 5:10
- ❸ The better agreement: 8:1–13
- ❹ No more sacrifice: 10:1–18
- ❺ Faith makes us sure: 11:1–40

Why does it matter?

Hebrews argues that Christianity is the fulfilment of Judaism. The rules and regulations have been superseded, the barriers torn down. The writer scrolls through centuries of Jewish history showing how its heroes have been characterized by faith. But even heroes such as Aaron, Moses, Abraham, and Joshua must bow to their superior, the one true high priest, Jesus Christ. He is our once-for-all sacrifice, offering salvation for everyone. All you need is faith.

Surprise me

The author is not known. Some people have suggested Barnabas, Luke, or even Apollos. Whoever he was, he knew Timothy (13:23). Martin Luther thought it was Apollos. But we just don't know.

Faith and works

Starring: James

What is it?

It's a revolutionary pamphlet. Down with the rich! Up with the workers! Well, up with the "good workers", anyway. Because this letter is about putting faith into action. It was written by the brother of Jesus and leader of the Jerusalem church, although, with true humility, he describes himself simply as a servant of God and of the Lord Jesus Christ.

What happens?

James reminds his audience to remain faithful as their faith is tested ❶. Those who endure temptation are blessed. Everyone should be quick to listen, slow to speak, and slow to anger. The key thing is to *do* the word, not just listen to it. Don't show favouritism to the rich. Love your neighbour as yourself ❷. Faith without works is dead. Your works reveal your faith. It's not enough just to believe in God – after all, even demons do that; a person is justified by what they do as well as by faith ❸.

It's important to tame the tongue and seek wisdom

JAMES

Don't show favouritism and mind your words. Just talking about faith is useless. Faith=works. Submit to God and put faith into practice.

from God. The evil cravings within us cause conflicts and disputes ❹. Instead of being a "friend of the world", we should submit ourselves to God. If we humble ourselves he will lift us up. Don't judge one another. Don't speak evil against one another. Don't boast about future plans: only God knows what will happen. And, as for you rich people who oppress your workers, the Lord is listening to their cries. The last days are coming ❺.

So, believers, wait patiently for the return of Jesus. Don't grumble; endure suffering; pray for those who are sick or in trouble. And, if anyone wanders away, do all you can to bring them back.

IN FIVE

❶ Trials: 1:1–18
❷ Look after the poor: 2:1–13
❸ Faith and works: 2:14–26
❹ Control your tongue: 3:1–18
❺ Why do you fight?: 4:1 – 5:6

Surprise me

His name is actually Jacob. (The letter begins "Iakob – a servant of God and of the Lord Jesus Christ…") For some reason, in English translations he's always called James.

Why does it matter?

The big theme of James is that faith has to be lived out. He champions the rights of the poor, criticizes snobs and bigots, and urges us to control our tongues. This emphasis on actions has led some to accuse James of not being "Christian" enough. But this letter actually contains more quotes from Christ than all the other New Testament letters put together. And James never says that actions are a substitute for faith; he says that if our faith doesn't result in practical, loving deeds then it's not real.

To the exiles

Starring: Peter and the Jewish Christian communities in Pontus, Galatia, Cappadocia, Asia, and Bithynia

What is it?

It's a letter for migrant workers. Or a newsletter for an ex-pat community. This is a circular letter to Christian Jews living in the Greco-Roman world. They are being marginalized and persecuted and Peter writes to strengthen and encourage them.

@ **1PETER**

It's no shame to be persecuted: it means you're being more like Christ. Keep on doing what's right. Trust God. He won't fail you.

What happens?

Peter greets Jewish Christian "exiles" in the Roman empire. God has given them a living hope through the resurrection of Jesus. The trials they are undergoing are purifying and perfecting their faith. Peter urges them to really love one another ❶. Having been given new life, they must put away hypocrisy, jealousy and backstabbing, and all that stuff. They are like living stones, being built into a holy building. And the cornerstone of this building is Jesus, the "stone the builders rejected" ❷.

The exiles are a chosen race, a royal priesthood. So they must live as servants of God and follow the example of Christ's suffering. Don't repay evil for evil. Don't be afraid. Respond to your opponents with gentleness and respect. Don't join in with pagan drunkenness and debauchery ❸. The end is coming, so take this stuff seriously. It's no surprise that you're being attacked. And, leaders, look after your flocks willingly and humbly, not for material gain. The God of all grace will give you strength and restoration.

IN THREE

❶ **Hope and endurance: 1:1–21**

❷ **Building something special: 1:22 – 2:10**

❸ **Don't be surprised: 3:13 – 4:6**

Surprise me

Peter says he is "in Babylon" (5:13). This is a Christian code word for Rome. Most likely, Peter wrote this letter in Rome in the mid-sixties AD, before the persecution of Christians by Emperor Nero.

Why does it matter?

Today, all around the world Christians are being persecuted. In places such as North Korea, Iran, Afghanistan, and Eritrea, the church is attacked, slandered, and abused. Christians are persecuted, imprisoned, and murdered. Peter is writing for people like this. In the kingdom of God, persecution comes with the territory. Peter turns everything on its head: he says it's a privilege to suffer for being a Christian!

Like a thousand years

@

2PETER

Stick to the true teaching. Remember the words of the prophets and the teachings of Jesus. Have patience: to God, a day is like 1,000 years.

☆

Starring: Peter

What is it?

It's an affidavit. Peter gives his own testimony in this one: "we were not making up clever stories…" he writes (1:16). He's actually seen this stuff. This is a man who saw the power of Jesus. And he's writing a final message to remind Christians to live in God's power and hold fast to his promises.

What happens?

Greetings from Simon Peter, a servant and apostle of Jesus Christ. Christ's divine power has given us all we need to escape from the corruption of the world and to do the things we know are right ❶. We don't follow a load of myths and make-believe, we were eyewitnesses of Christ's majesty. We heard God himself honour and glorify Jesus while we were with him on that mountain. So the message of the prophets is confirmed. And they received their messages not from humans, but from God ❷.

As for false teachers and prophets, they will be punished, just like God punished the rebellious angels, or the rest of the world during the time of Noah. These teachers are self-indulgent, irrational, and determined to slander what they don't understand. They are dry springs, wind-blown mists. They speak nonsense. The Lord is on his way, but with the Lord one day is like a thousand years (and vice versa). The day of the Lord will come like a thief in the night. All we can do is lead lives of holiness and godliness and wait patiently.

Listen to what Paul says (although some things in his letters are a bit difficult to understand) ❸.

Why does it matter?

False teaching is coming into the church. People are taking the words of others – for example, Paul's letters – and twisting them to suit their own ends. They hold out promises of freedom, but they themselves are "slaves of depravity" (2:19). Some even deny that Jesus is coming, but Peter argues that God's timetable is not the same as ours.

IN THREE

1. **All we need: 1:1–15**
2. **Christ's glory: 1:16–21**
3. **The Lord's return: 3:1–17**

Surprise me

Peter refers to reading letters by Paul (3:15–16). And he agrees that some parts are hard to understand!

Love, actually

What is it?

It's a certificate of authenticity. Or advice for an expert about how to tell whether something is the real thing. John is writing to combat false teaching. He tells his readers how they can be sure of their status as children of God and how the only test of true Christianity is whether the people demonstrate the love of Christ.

@ **1JOHN**

`If you don't show love, you don't know God. The only proof of authentic believers is whether they love. Don't just say it; do it. God=love.`

What happens?

We've seen the truth, heard it, touched it, and this is our testimony. This is the message: God is light, and in him there is no darkness at all. So, if we say that we belong to him and then carry on walking in the darkness we're just liars. But if we walk in the light we have fellowship with each other and Jesus' blood washes our sins away. We've all sinned, but, if we confess, he forgives us. He is our advocate; his sacrifice has saved us all ❶. The way we show we know him is by obeying his commands. If we live in Jesus, we walk as he walked. Don't love the things of this world: those things pass away, but those who obey God live for ever ❷.

☆ **Starring: John, the antichrists, and the false teachers**

It's the last hour! The final countdown! John warns that time is running short. There are what he calls "antichrists": liars, people who deny God and Jesus. The Father loves us; we are God's children now. When Jesus is revealed we will be like him and see him as he really is. You know who God's children are by their actions. We should love one another, not just in words but in actions. This reassures us of God's love. We should love each other as he loved us ❸.

Love is from God. If you don't love, you don't know God. God loved us so much that he sent his Son to die for us: so we ought to love one another. You can't say you love God and then hate your brother or sister ❹. We know we love God when we obey his commandments. God gave us eternal life and this life is in his Son. If we have him, then we have life ❺.

IN FIVE

- ❶ **Live in the light: 1:1 – 2:2**
- ❷ **Authentic believers: 2:3–17**
- ❸ **Children of God: 3:1–24**
- ❹ **God is love: 4:1–21**
- ❺ **Be sure: 5:1–21**

Surprise me

The false teachers John was writing about were probably Gnostics – people who promised special, secret knowledge. Their name comes from the Greek word *gnosis*, meaning "knowledge".

Why does it matter?

John is writing about false faith and false teachers. These people promised secret knowledge to their "initiates". But John says it's all very simple: you know who is a true child of God by their actions. That is the real proof of who are God's children. Not special knowledge or secret ideas, but love and obedience.

Live in the truth

What is it?

It's a disciplinary procedure. John writes about some leaders who have caused a split in the Christian community. In 2 John he encourages the followers to avoid false teachers. In 3 John he writes to a follower called Gaius, promising that he will come to sort out the split caused by a troublemaker named Diotrephes.

Starring: John, the "lady" and her children, Gaius, Diotrephes, and Demetrius

@ **2&3JOHN**

```
Love one another.
Avoid false
teachers; take care
of the true ones.
Can't write more
now. Will come soon
to sort things out.
```

What happens?

2 John begins with John greeting a lady and her children. He is overjoyed to find some of the children walking in the truth. He urges them to love one another and to show it by obeying God's commandments. Some people are denying that Jesus was a real, physical being. He writes that they're the antichrist, so the Christian community shouldn't have anything to do with them. He was going to write more, but now he intends to make a visit ❶.

3 John starts with John greeting Gaius. He is overjoyed at reports of Gaius' faithfulness. Nothing brings him more joy than to hear of his children walking in the truth. He urges Gaius to look after visiting "brothers" and support them ❷. Diotrephes has refused to acknowledge John's authority or show hospitality to the true brothers. John will come and sort things out. He writes that whoever does good comes from God; whoever does evil has not seen God. Also stating that Demetrius is one of the good guys. He ends with a hope to see Gaius soon ❸.

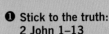

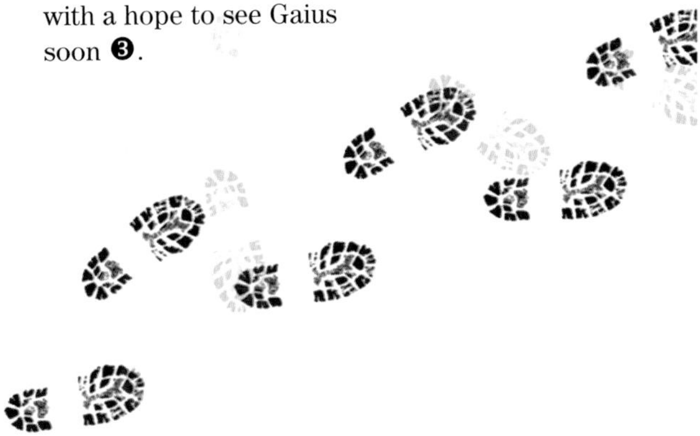

IN THREE

- ❶ **Stick to the truth: 2 John 1–13**
- ❷ **Work it out: 3 John 1–12**
- ❸ **I'll be there soon: 3 John 13–14**

Surprise me !

2 John is addressed to a "chosen lady and her children". This is probably a church, rather than an individual. Also at the end of the letter he refers to "the children of your chosen sister" – her sister church, as it were.

Why does it matter?

Love must be discerning. John argues against a naïve, "everyone welcome" approach, which was actually damaging the church. Jesus' true followers are those who "walk in the truth" (3 John 3–4).

Beware! False teaching!

What is it?

It's an urgent rewrite, in the sense that Jude originally planned to write about salvation, but has been forced to concentrate on defending the truth against false teachers. The book is attributed to Jude (or Judas), brother of James and Jesus (Matthew 13:55; Mark 6:3). He encourages believers to stay strong in the faith and to reject false teaching and failing leadership.

@ JUDE
Defend the truth! Don't be fooled by fruitless teaching and unsettling lies. God can keep you steady and bring you home.

Starring: Jude, Enoch, and Michael

What happens?

From Jude, a servant of Christ and James' brother. He was planning to write them a letter about salvation, but has had to change tack. Certain "intruders" have infiltrated the church: people who pervert the grace of God. These false teachers will receive judgment (illustrated by historical figures such as Cain, Balaam, and the citizens of Sodom and Gomorrah). These people defile the church's special meals. They are like clouds without rain, fruitless trees in autumn, wild waves, wandering stars: all noise and bluster. They grumble and moan, indulge themselves, flatter people to gain an advantage.

But this was prophesied by the apostles of Jesus as a sign of the end times. They warned us that there would be worldly people like this. So keep faithful. Pray in the Holy Spirit and trust to the mercy of Christ. Have mercy on those who are tempted: save those you can ❶.

Finally Jude ends with a magnificent prayer to Christ, the authority now and always.

IN ONE

❶ Remember what you've been told: 1–25.

Surprise me

Jude draws not only on Old Testament writings, but also on non-biblical books called *1 Enoch* and *The Testament of Moses*.

Why does it matter?

Jude warns us that what we say and do has consequences (and especially what we teach). False teachers who sow division will be judged. Jude shows a powerful command of language. He describes these divisive teachers as waterless clouds, fruitless trees, wandering stars, and wild, foaming waves. And he closes with one of the most moving prayers in the New Testament.

Apocalypse now

@ REVELATION
`I've seen the future: God wins.`

What is it?

You know those political cartoons where the lion stands for Britain and the bear for Russia and the eagle for America? Well, Revelation is a bit like that. It's a vision full of symbols and pictures. It's an epic, anti-imperial, apocalyptic tract. It's a series of letters to various churches. All of this goes to show that the only word that really describes Revelation is "indescribable".

☆

Starring: John, Jesus, the Holy One, Michael and various angels, the beast from the sea, the beast from the pit, the dragon, the lady, the whore of Babylon, and another beast. Introducing the New Heaven and the New Earth. And featuring Jerusalem as "the Bride"

What happens?

John is on Patmos when he sees a vision ❶. He turns to see a figure "like a son of man", who gives John messages addressed to the "angels" of seven churches in the Roman province of Asia (modern western Turkey) ❷.

After this John sees a being seated on a throne, surrounded by worshipping creatures, and holding a scroll with seven seals. A lamb (with seven horns and seven eyes) opens the seals one by one ❸. The first four seals release a succession of riders on horses; the fifth shows the souls of persecution victims crying out for judgment. The sixth releases many natural disasters ❹. When the seventh seal is opened there is silence in heaven.

Seven angels arrive with seven trumpets. The first four trumpets release disasters onto the earth. The fifth trumpet blast leads to the opening of a bottomless pit, from which come locusts ❺. The sixth trumpet releases four angels who kill a third of humankind, but the "elect" are saved. After the seventh trumpet blast, a voice proclaims the reign of "our Lord and his messiah". A pregnant, crowned woman is threatened by a dragon. Her baby is taken to heaven. Michael defeats the dragon, who subsequently makes war on those who keep God's commandments. The dragon is joined by a beast from the sea. This beast is joined by another beast from the earth ❻.

John sees seven angels with seven bowls, each of which releases different disasters ❼. He sees a whore sitting on a scarlet beast. Babylon, the great city, is destroyed, leading to rejoicing in heaven ❽. There is a great battle when the beast's army is defeated. An angel seals the dragon in a pit for a thousand years ❾. (He will be released, but ultimately destroyed.) Then God judges the dead and creates a new heaven and a new earth where "those who overcome" will live with God for ever in the new Jerusalem.

Finally, John is told that Jesus will return soon. There are warnings not to tamper with the book or edit it in any way ❿.

IN TEN

10

- ❶ The vision: 1:1–20
- ❷ Letters to churches: 2:1 – 3:22
- ❸ The throne and the Lamb: 4:1 – 5:14
- ❹ Seven seals: 6:1–17
- ❺ Seven trumpets: 8:1 – 9:21
- ❻ Woman and beasts: 12:1 – 13:18
- ❼ Seven bowls: 16:1–21
- ❽ Fall of Babylon: 18:1 – 19:10
- ❾ Satan's downfall: 19:11 – 20:10
- ❿ New heaven and new earth: 20:11 – 22:21

Why does it matter?

Revelation was written at a time when churches were facing persecution by Rome, the great imperial power. But the message of Revelation is: "These powers don't really have the victory." The book gives a vision of the future, in which Christ is triumphant, not the powers of the world. Whoever is in charge at the moment, whichever petty worldly power thinks it has the victory, in the end, God wins.

Surprise me

It's not actually John's Revelation. It was actually given to Jesus, who passed it on. The opening lines read, "The revelation of Jesus Christ, which God gave him to show his servants…" (1:1).